Pages Off
The
Doctor's Pad

Harold C. Klein, M.D.

6/19/95

To:
John + Shirley =
Our new found

friends :

Pages Off the Doctor's Pad

by Harold C. Klein, M.D.

Published by Lakeside Press
5124 Mayfield Road, #191
Cleveland, Ohio 44124

To order the book call toll-free 1-800-247-6553

Publisher's Cataloging in Publication
(Prepared by Quality Books Inc.)

Klein, Harold C.
  Pages off the doctor's pad / by Harold C. Klein.
  p.   cm.
  Preassigned LCCN: 93-79811.
  ISBN 1-879653-07-9

  1. Klein, Harold C.   2. Physicians—United States—Biography.
3. Sick—Psychology.   4. Physician and patient.   I. Title.

R154.K54K54   1994   610.695'2'092
                                              QBI93-21758

To my Miriam. . . .

   Who shares my bed. . . .
my brain. . . . . my being. She
shaped these words and
made them sing.

                                      H. C. K.

Contents

Introduction

Doctoring the sick is a profession as old and established as harlotry. Both have succeeded in soothing. Neither has ever been able to cure.

Our surgical brothers have always been a group apart. With their needles and knives they could lance a boil, excise an inflamed appendix, repair a rupture or remove a stone-sick gall bladder. We medical professionals, on the other hand—prior to the advent of antibiotics a mere fifty years ago—could only listen, attend, advise and try to do no harm.

Even with limited therapeutic tools, I, as an internist, have found great satisfaction in this relatively primal mission of caring for the sick. I chose the practice of medicine because it is more than tagging names to symptoms and then applying the proper poultice or prescribing the proper pill. It is being sensitive to the complexity of the person within the ailing body; the fears, foibles, frailties, fantasies that are buried in silence beneath the physical complaints that are so articulate in their cries for help.

It has always fascinated me that—just as patients disrobe into examining gowns without any hesitation—so do they shed their facades and hang them on the hooks with their clothes. Be it their respect for medical training and experience or the mystique that seems to deify the profession, people do bare themselves to their doctors. And in this communication there are family histories and stories—some relevant to their aches and pains, some not. Some trickle out

1

as confidences. Some pour out as confessions. Most, however, illumine the patients' problems so clearly that it may only take an understanding ear and a guiding hand to reassure and lead the ill back to health.

And stories about doctors are intriguing too, but we hesitate to diagnose each other—at least publicly. Many of these have grown into gospel or legend through the decades. Others that are more in-house gossip are embroidered and recycled with the changing of the house staffs and remain privy only to the profession.

And there are paramedical stories and personal observations that fill other pages of my scrapbook. These I have long wanted to leaf through—to cull out—to share—and—just to muse. . . .

1

The Classical Case

"A classical case". That's what the psychiatrist called it. He documented his diagnosis in a detailed letter to me prescribing a trial of psychotherapy—with the caution that an extended course of analysis might be necessary later.

The "classic case" was that of a man we can call "John". From his first visit to my office John bewildered me. I cannot tell you why. Maybe it's the way he told his story. Some patients reel off their symptoms without emotion—in grocery list fashion—while others kind of act out, making you feel their every little twinge right along with them. That was John. His account was charged with anguish, a pathetic voice begging for relief. He didn't just complain about his devastating headaches, he had me sharing the pain that was destroying his life and turning his world inside out.

There was nothing particularly prominent about John—in either manner or mien. He was 42, an average 5 foot 9, 165 pounder without a single feature to distinguish him. In both personality and complexion he was elephant gray and his clothes seemed to be chosen to match. His hair was skimpy—neither straight nor curly—but also gray. Actually, his faded blue eyes and the red neckties his wife was forever buying for him were the only variables in this monochromatic man.

John had been trudging his way through life in a pedestrian pattern of maximal apathy and minimal accomplishment. Although he had acquired a law degree, he made his

3

living as a plumbing supply salesman. He seemed satisfied enough with his marriage and his two healthy children. During the past year, for no apparent reason, he developed a series of headaches that had become increasingly frequent and severe. An aspirin or two used to do the trick, he told me, but now it took three or four at a time for even a measure of relief. What was so odd was that the attacks were sporadic—sometimes coming on daily and sometimes not for three or four days—but always without forecast. Although they lasted only a few minutes, they would trigger a sense of something ominous about to happen and that threw him into a panic. Even more odd, they most frequently came in the morning while he was shaving. With or without aspirin, the headaches would slowly fade out and then completely disappear by the time he was dressed and ready to leave for work. John and I talked about this strange association with his morning shave, but neither of us could figure it out. I quizzed him at length about medications, exposure to toxic substances at home and at work, and about sensitivity to food or other allergens. There were no clues.

Not only did I find nothing abnormal in my complete examination, but the laboratory studies were equally nonproductive. On the basis of these double negatives, I was cornered into the discomfort that is so frustrating to a physician—of having to resort to reassurance and a change of pain medication as my only therapeutic options. I asked him to stay in touch, and that he did. On each of his frequent return visits, he reported less response to my medicines and more headaches. I, in turn, became more oppressed by my diagnostic failure. John tried desparately to make me understand how very frightened he was, and one day when his wife came with him, she echoed his panic. "Doctor, you have to understand. These aren't just headaches. He's in excruciating pain. He squeezes his head between his hands, the sweat pours off him, and his eyes bulge like he's looking at death. When the children see him like that, they scream and run to their rooms. You have to see him in an attack to believe what I'm telling you. We just can't go on like this. You have to find a way to help my husband."

I couldn't go on like this either. I decided to admit him to the hospital for more exotic testing, but above all, for on site observation. My hope was that if he could be caught in an attack by a trained professional—an intern or a nurse —some significant data might be recorded. It was a great idea, but Nature can be a tricky adversary. In the hospital, between stress tests, cardiac monitors, brain waves, and every other pertinent procedure, John walked the corridors for four solid days symptom-free. No clinical findings, no positive tests, and—most frustrating—no headaches. We even had him shave three times each day to substantiate that mysterious association. Zero! I finally discharged him with the diagnosis, "Headache, cause undetermined", and that was when I referred him to the psychiatrist who subsequently identified John as a classic case of functional illness. His aforementioned report to me was the case history of a severely disturbed man, emotionally injured by the conflicts of his early life. Reading like pages out of Freud, this was the story.

John's father, a big bull of a man who drove a truck in the inner city, was endowed with all the unsavory attributes ascribed to truck drivers as a class. His mother was a delicately built asthenic woman who had earned a teacher's diploma, but had abandoned her career early in her first pregnancy. There were three siblings. The two older brothers were chips off the paternal block—husky young bruisers and strong competitive athletes. The baby sister was a clone of her mother—short on grace, strength, and motivation—just a colorless little girl.

John, lacking the athletic aptitude of his brothers, survived his tough teen years in this incompatible environment via escape to the mesmery of his books—in the refuge of fiction and fantasy. Despite a lackluster school record, he did manage to get through his courses and eventually, financed by part-time work, achieved what he thought had been his lifelong ambition—a degree in law. That academic accomplishment, however, brought no applause from his family. All through his student years John suffered the double indignity of being unable to compete in a sports-oriented male society and having to be audience to his brothers' triumphs. How painful it was to have to sit in the stands with his father cheering his brothers' victories, and then endure the replay at the dinner table. And those brothers never passed up a chance to hit him where he hurt. Worst of all, when he tried to escape to the solace of his reading, they would taunt him cruelly and then play catch with his precious books. Some day, he swore he would get even. Some day! He just knew he would! For the present, he had to find comfort in a series of repetitive dreams—seeing himself as a successful trial lawyer strutting confidently before an attentive jury—weaving a lurid case before a raptured gallery where his adoring mother, his father and his brothers sat.

In reality, John had started his career as a clerk in a three-man office that specialized in real estate law—a dull job that fell far short of the challenge he had anticipated. The only break in the tedium of his workaday world was a romance with a secretary in another office down the hall. It began with impromptu lunches and then matriculated into real dates. But, as they saw more of each other, the excitement dissipated into the humdrum. The secretary's work was stultifying and poor pay. The young lawyer's was equally boring and barely covered his rent. After much sad and shared soul searching, John tabled his hopes of a brilliant courtroom career for what seemed to be the financial advantages of a salesman for his fiancee's brother's company. It was that employment that licensed the betrothed to the altar.

In the beginning, the newlyweds were happily preoccupied making love, making children, making a home. John tried to keep his dreams alive, but as the years slipped away, his problems grew with the children and their expanding needs. The promising position was better financially, but soon dwindled into a drone of tedium and limitation. He hated the demeaning routine of day to day dealing with the low-class demanding plumbers who were his customers, and he resented his boss brother-in-law's coarse sense of humor. He was chained to a peg and had to pace his little circle—round and round—just to eke out his daily needs. The reveries of his law school days became fainter—yet more haunting. He could find no exit and his shabby compromise seemed stuck in his craw.

Each morning when he opened his eyes, there was the dreaded prospect of another day at his loathesome job. And, as the psychiatrist pinpointed in his letter, it was when he was alone in the bathroom, looking at himself in the mirror while shaving, that he had to see himself honestly reflected in the blinding light of self defeat. This was a portrait he could not accept. The pain of frustration and failure translated into the blinding headache. The manifestation was pat and perfect—classical reasons for the psychiatrist's diagnosis of a functional type of headache. The proof of the pudding, he assured me, was that after a few airing-out analytic sessions, the headaches became less frequent, and, when they did appear, were much more tolerable.

In my practice I have always tried to avoid making a "functional" diagnosis. To me, that's a cop-out—a wastebasket diagnosis. When a surgeon is back-walled for a solid answer, he may jokingly say, "When in doubt, cut it out". Medical people, on the other hand, often label a case "functional", meaning that it is a disease of a function of the body, not of its structure, and then trash it with pat phrases: "You're too tense". "You're wound up too tight". "Your watch has all the right wheels but it just doesn't keep good time". And that may transfer the blame from the doctor's inadequacy to the patient's. In John's case, however, no matter how we labeled the illness, he *was* getting better and *that* was the bottom line.

And so, during the weeks that passed, I presumed he was being comfortably councilled to recovery on the psychiatrist's couch. Then, early one morning while I was still sleeping, the harsh ring of the telephone pierced my bubble. It was John's wife pleading hysterically, "Doctor, come now! Please! Now!"

That was in the days when we doctors made house calls and often in the middle of the night. My wife used to rib me for meticulously laying out the tired clothes I'd worn that day so they'd be ready at any hour—just in case. This was a "just in case" that cut my response time to minutes. John's wife was waiting at the front door of their small suburban home. She grabbed my arm and rushed me to the bathroom. There was John—clutching the sink to support himself—heaving in deep struggling respirations—his eyes red and bulging. He was in a devil's grip. He said nothing but his panic was articulate. I reached for his pulse. It was bounding and pounding away at a very rapid rate. The arteries on his temples—sinuous and snake-like—were beating out their own tattoo. I quickly opened my bag, dug out the blood pressure cuff and wrapped it around his arm. Then—at that instant—I knew it all! A pheo! This had to be a pheo! It had to be! His systolic pressure was higher than my machine could register—over 300, and his diastolic was 160. These were killing pressures! He looked ready to explode. Only a tumor of the adrenal gland could secrete the amount of adrenalin necessary to abruptly shoot his blood pressure up that high—high enough to blow out a vital coronary or cerebral vessel and snuff him out in the snap of a finger.

Somehow, we got into my car. With one hand on the wheel and the other monitoring John's pulse, I raced wildly to the hospital, all the time hoping that I wouldn't be stopped in this mad sprint against time. What seemed like an eternity later, John was on an emergency room cart with a Regitine drip going into his vein. Within minutes his blood pressure started to slack off and John began to look human, but that was only a temporary surcease. There still was much to be done.

With this breather the total picture came into focus. John apparently had a rare tumor—one that is almost invariably fatal because it can secrete large amounts of adrenalin when it is active and unrestricted by any of the checks and balances of normal glandular physiology. It was like a boiler being fired up way beyond its safe limits. When the tumor was quiescent, just sitting in situ for long periods and not pouring adrenalin into the circulation, there was no way to detect it or even suspect it. Now there was no question. The tumor was there and it had to come out, but how soon? That depended on if or when the monster would stop its spree. So far it had not. Whenever we tried to slow the Regitine drip, the heart began to pound again and the pressure would start to rise.

My first move was to call in a topnotch surgeon and brief him on John's story. "A pheo! Holy Moses!" He glowed with excitement. It was not every day that he saw a case like this. Sudden death on the operating table was more than a mere possibility but I was confident that my surgeon was up to all of it. The x-rays he ordered to determine which side to attack showed us the little bandit sitting astride the right kidney. It was only the size of a small plum, but a ruthless killer. It was hard to believe that that faint little shadow could have been what had been tormenting John and baffling me all these months.

That done, we hurried off to the library to update ourselves on the latest statistics on pheos. Despite its rarity, there had been much interest in this tumor and much had been written. My recollection was that most of the literature had been pessimistic, but I couldn't hang a man's life on my memory and there was always the outside chance that something new had been published that could help us.

Only 270 cases had been reported thus far in the medical literature and in two-thirds of them, the diagnosis had not been made until the patient reached the autopsy table. Of the other 90 patients, only 15 had been saved by surgery. The others had died either before an operation could be attempted or on the table. These numbers shook us up, but still we knew we had no choice.

Timing was now becoming essential. Our tests had consumed many hours and the day was winding down. It was obvious that the tumor had not expended itself and its continuous spout put a gun to our heads. We just couldn't depend on the reining effect of the Regitine drip much longer. After a quick final conference with doctors and staff and a strained review with John and his wife, the decision was made. We had to dig that marauder out tonight. Nurses, operating room, anesthesia, instruments, and staff—all were readied by a series of staccato orders. A strong sedative was surreptitiously slipped into John's intravenous tube to allay any further stress, and then the procession to the operating room took off. Orderlies pushed the cart bearing the groggy, drowsing patient with dangling I.V.s dripping into each of his arms. Alongside, his teary-eyed, terrified wife was brushing his lips with hers at every pause on the route. It was midnight—a long, long 18 hours after that urgent morning house call.

Surgery like this can be nerve-wracking and everyone in the O.R., each an expert in his field, was sensitive to the specific hazards. They knew that unchecked, the tumor had been making more than enough adrenalin for both glands so that the normal left-sided one, unneeded, had become freed to shut down the production of its cells and idle away in hibernation. It was anyone's guess how long it had been asleep, and how long it would take to get the gland awake and back into operation. We did know that when the surgeon clamped off the vessels of the tumorous gland to shut off its supply of adrenalin to the body, the reaction could be fatal. We had to be ready to immediately supply the vital hormone and maintain its flow for as long as it took for the sleeping left adrenal to start functioning. We also knew that this type of tumor was like a sponge, soaked and full of adrenalin ready to fire. The slightest pressure on that loaded pistol could send a lethal flood into the bloodstream. One wrong move—one missed signal—and it would be out of our hands. These hands were ready—trained—tense—but ready.

Making the long sweeping incision was like drawing back a red velvet curtain on a strange melodrama, and with it, there was a hush in the audience. Once the abdomen was entered, bleeders tied off, sponges removed and counted, it was all hands out except for the surgeon. Only he could be trusted to handle the nimble dissection needed to safely expose the tumor. No one ever stalked a quarry more stealthily than he, threading his way through the varying tissues— snipping, spreading, cutting ever so carefully—working a path down to the right kidney. All eyes focussed on his motions. All ears tuned to the tempo of the beep–beep–beep of the cardiac monitor. With each sudden acceleration of the beats, our breaths were caught up in our own palpitations of apprehension. To the surgeon it was a signal to stop, withdraw, shoot a questioning look to the anesthetist and wait for her nod and a return to the normal play of the pulses. After an endless succession of pauses and attacks, the tumor was finally isolated and exposed.

Now the surgeon could step back, slowly rinse the blood off his gloves and collect himself. That was it. The time had come to play out the last climactic act. Slowly and meticulously, his hands re-entered the abdomen and went back to work. With ultra fastidious dissection, he edged his clamps around the adrenal vessels and, when they were placed to his satisfaction, he straightened up and tensely announced, "Ready". Turning his head to face each assistant in the room, he asked, "Ready?" Each in turn echoed their answers, "Ready", "Ready", "Ready". Then, like a general moving his men, he barked out, "Let's go!" In that same moment, one could hear the rasping sound made by the closing of the arterial clamp followed by the clamp on the vein. The sounds sent the operating room corps jumping into action.

"Regitine off".

"Adrenalin on—sixty drops per minute".

Clamping the adrenal vessels had effectively turned off the faucet on his flow of adrenalin and now, it was up to the team to replace it—but at a controlled rate—as many drops per minute as his body required. Now at last, the stopcock was in our control.

"No pressure! No pressure!", warned the anesthetist.

"Heart rate?"

"Twenty—very thready".

I felt under the sheets for his pulse. There was none! Peering behind the headshield, I could see John's face. Dead gray! No pulse. No pressure. By medical criteria our patient was dead.

Scurrying nurses were repeating orders, filling syringes, giving injections, and regulating the intravenous solutions— all accompanied by the rhythmic huff-puff of the anesthetist's gas balloon. In the midst of all this traffic and turmoil, only the surgeon was still—statue still—and silent. Only his eyes moved—peering, darting, penetrating every segment of the battle he was commanding. Arms folded across his chest, his very solid presence in the midst of the action dictated the direction, the flow, and maintained the urgency of the moment.

Seconds dragged their feet while we waited breathlessly for our adrenalin to bring John back to life. At last, hesitant bleeps started coming through the monitors and, as they began to strengthen and quicken, a pressure slowly formed. Beat by beat and step by hesitant step, our man was inching his way back from the graveyard. Soon he had a pulse— barely palpable—but a pulse I could feel, and then, with color beginning to come back to his face, I knew he had made the turn. He was going to make it. In this room—in this sterile little enclave—in the still and dark of the night— while the whole world was asleep—confluent rivulets of knowledge, training and talent had flowed together to make a stream of power that saved the life of a man.

Removing the tumor now would be a routine surgical procedure so I slipped out of the operating room, down the hall and into the little waiting room where I had isolated his wife away from the rest of the family. She rushed into my arms and I held her and let her sob out her relief and her gratitude. What an ecstatic moment that was for me—the acme of gratification that for a flick of time compensates for all the periods of trauma that punctuate the professional life of a physician.

In three days we were able to pull his tubes, and in a week John was eating, walking and begging to go home. He made his triumphal discharge on the tenth day, leaving his headaches drowning in the same formaldehyde that was safely storing his tumor in a specimen bottle on a shelf of the pathology lab.

Some months later the "Pheo Case" was featured in the Hospital's Medical Grand Rounds. It was a unique and titillating thrill to sit in a back row and listen to the review of my case. Our chief was the presenter and, although I heard his every word, I was really floating in a sea of memories that had made this case one of the most fascinating pages in my medical scrapbook. Yes, I did hear—"Pheochromocytoma . . . very rare disease . . . fascinating physiology . . . bursts of adrenalin . . . coming without fixed intervals . . . high mortality rate . . . fatal accidents of the heart and brain before it can be discovered . . . diagnostic tests are often deceptive . . . treatment is always surgical . . . and so . . . this was a classical example . . . a 'classic case'. "

Classic case? Indeed! But that's what the psychiatrist called it too.

There were so many aspects of John's history that couldn't be presented that day—lingering unanswered questions that I still find need to mull over. I knew that it was the poverty of organic findings and the wealth of emotional material in John's background that detoured me into the psychiatric approach. Like the forest-wise Indian who would try to glean the who, what and why of an abandoned campsite by just poking around in its ashes, so we physicians often rake the rubble of a patient's past in an effort to unearth valuable clues to his present problems. Unfortunately, there are times when what we unearth can be as deceptive as profitable. In John's case I certainly was lured by a false scent until it was almost too late.

That his wife chose that day to tumble me out of bed—that particular day—the day the tumor had become ripe enough to fire its killing blast was sheer good fortune. The random periodicity of its previous adrenalin squirts must be ascribed to the nature of the growth and whatever inexplicable stimuli triggered them. And what of the timing with his shaves? I could only conjecture that it could have been the prolonged standing that might have allowed the kidney to sag in the abdomen, thereby producing enough tension or pressure on the tumor to eject its load—enough adrenalin to shoot up his blood pressure and produce a whopping headache. Perhaps.

John's improvement with the analytic therapy? That might be easier to explain, falling in line with the dictum that almost all illness is exacerbated by tension and alleviated by relaxation. Perhaps.

The man we have called "John" still works for his brother-in-law. He still sells plumbing supplies. He still dreams of being a practicing attorney. He still shaves in front of his mirror every morning. But—he no longer gets headaches. He was a classic case.

2

The Toothpick Surgeon

You ask why some of us call our Chief of Surgery, "Toothpicks Carlone"? That's a story all of its own.

As surgeons go, Rocco Carlone was a pip. Respected for his knife-sharp judgement and his superb, innate dexterity, he was always in demand and he was always busy. He could make the most complicated bowel resection or deep common bile duct repair look as easy as a simple appendix. And he was fast. His motto was, "less time, less trauma," and his patients seemed to benefit thereby. All the guys knew that if an assistant took too long to dress and scrub, he would find the operation over by the time he arrived at the table. And, every so often, when a lesser surgeon found himself backed into a tight corner, unable to accomplish what needed to be done, Carlone got an SOS to scrub in. With a quick look, a nod of the head, a few adroit maneuvers, somehow he'd get the stitch placed and the bleeding stemmed. Then the operation could proceed.

Although he was a surgeon's surgeon, out of his scrub suit—his appearance belied his calling. He wore good enough clothes, yet he usually looked as though he'd dressed in the dark. His jacket was a little askew, his tie a little aslant, and when he was at rest, his body slouched into a sloppy stance. Never his eyes! I could not picture Carlone with his eyes closed, even asleep. When he was operating, everything seemed to be in motion—quick, staccato motion. His hands, arms, body all became a team with his piercing, excited eyes. There was speed and precision. His cadence picked up everyone around him so that moving with measured tread in his proximity was like trying to amble on Main Street during rush hour. It just could not be done.

As with many new Americans, Rocco had had his hurdles. He was a twelve-year old when his family immigrated from a small Tuscan village to settle in our own "Little Italy." Despite his most earnest efforts at mimicking the American born kids, to this day the faint trace of his birth tongue still clings to him and flavors his speech.

With the tender warmth so common to his race, he couldn't bear hearing about a patient's pain or distress. Although postoperative discomfort in an incision was an acceptable norm to him, Rocco couldn't tolerate hearing that "it hurt." Pain was a word, a thing that he refused to accept emotionally. His ears may have accepted the cry of pain but they never let it get through to his brain.

Like so many surgeons, he had no patience with the documenting and verbiage of complaints. There was neither room nor time for dalliance once he made a decision. His concern was the meat of the problem—never the garnish. His history-taking was always succinct and abbreviated. With incisive and piercing questions, he would invariably cut off the rambling side issues people tend to use to embroider the essentials. If that amputation didn't do the trick, he was known to turn his back on the patient and—without a whisper of explanation—walk out of the room. (Perhaps that's what separates the surgeons from the internists who feel a commitment to hear out the most minute and often irrelevant meanderings of patients. And maybe it is that distinction that steers medical students and interns into the surgical specialties where they can work in the purely technical aspects of medicine—unencumbered and undistracted by the human element.)

So often the story is retold of how, during his surgical residency some 25 years earlier, he had been awakened early one morning by a call from the interne on emergency room duty. It seems that three creative fraternity brothers from the university campus nearby thought up a rather bizarre hazing stunt. They shoved a flashlight into a freshman's anus so he could run around the dormitories "lighting up the world." Unfortunately, in their drunken exuberance, their little firecracker backfired. They had rammed the two celled light too far and no way could they get it out. The poor victim was soon in agony and the jokesters, in panic, rushed him to the emergency room. The interne knew immediately that they needed the relaxation of a general anesthetic to safely remove the foreign body, and that's when he called Carlone for help.

Listening to the story on the phone, Rocco was convinced that the interne was having his own little joke.

"Did you say a flashlight in da rectum?"

"That's what I said."

"Is da flashlight lit?"

"Yes, as a matter of fact, it *is* lit."

"Then turn it off, you dummy," he snapped, "don't you know that in da rectum it's gotta be dark!", and slammed the receiver back into its cradle.

After a third call, Rocco was finally convinced this was no hoax. He painfully dragged himself out of bed and down to the emergency room to assist in the removal of the obstructing flashlight. That's the end of the story, but Carlone's quip has lived on in the lore of the hospital staff all these years—"in da rectum it's gotta be dark."

Another Carlone story involved me and it started with a phone call that interrupted the delicious leisure of a Sunday off service. It was Herb Boyer, an internist on our staff. He apologized for disturbing me on the weekend, but went on to tell me that earlier that day he had admitted a patient who had him very concerned. No, it couldn't hold 'til morning. Sensing the urgency in his voice, I had no choice but to meet him at the hospital for a consultation.

When I got there, Herb briefed me on the case. The man was 73, had been a long-time patient who had always enjoyed good health except for some low grade hypertension—not serious enough to be treated. With his wife, a brother and sister-in-law he had just returned from a month at the same hotel in Oaxaca, Mexico where they had vacationed for the past ten years. Although he had been feeling a little below par during their last week in Mexico, it had not been severe enough to warrant aborting their holiday.

Early that Sunday morning, two days since his return, he was awakened by severe, boring, toothachey pain in the right side of his abdomen that seemed to press through to his right shoulder blade. He became nauseated and tried to vomit, but to no avail. That's when his wife called Dr. Boyer who arranged to meet them in the emergency room.

On examination, Herb told me, he had first noticed a jaundiced tinge to the man's skin and yet, his eyes did not look yellow. His whole abdomen was distended and tender, but most marked over a moderately enlarged liver. He had a fever of 101 degrees and his laboratory reports were equivocal. The white blood cell count was a little elevated and the liver function tests were neither normal nor high enough to be specific. Blood cultures and serologic tests had been drawn, but those wouldn't come through for several days. Herb had wisely asked if any other member of the family had been similarly ill but no one had. He was also assured that the group had always exercised the utmost caution about the water, fresh fruits and vegetables in Mexico and just as assiduously, had avoided all shell fish during their annual trips.

Herb was distressed by nagging doubts and subtle possibilities. Although he had admitted his patient to a private room under strict isolation with the diagnosis of hepatitis, he realized he could be dealing with an obstructed gall bladder full of stones. If this were indeed a case of gangrene of the gall bladder where a fatal rupture could occur, immediate surgery would be strongly indicated. If, however, it were hepatitis, the anesthesia of an operation would pose a terrible hazard to a sick liver. Herb had shared his dilemma with the family and they agreed to the urgent need for a consultant. That's how I entered this blurred confusing picture.

Herb introduced me to the patient and his in-laws who, in mid February, certainly were a healthy looking bunch with their fine Mexican tans. All except the patient—his color looked more icteric than suntan. I asked a few more questions and then, (like a true specialist), did my own palpations, rectal exam plus testing the stool for occult blood. It was all pretty much as Herb had described except that I was very impressed with the tenseness of the abdominal wall, the localized tenderness over the gall bladder area and the rebound jump of pain when I released my hand from its pressure on the belly wall. From my findings, I was convinced this man's problem was an obstructed, gangrenous gall bladder and that he urgently needed surgical relief.

We walked out into the hall to talk things over. I gave Herb my impressions. He still was unwavering in his diagnosis of hepatitis. We shared our differences with the family and the patient and discussed the hazards involved in proceeding on a wrong decision. The air in the room seemed to be choking all of us. How could laymen understand that even in this day and age, with all the advancements in medicine, it was possible for two top notch physicians to view one disease in directly opposing light? We finally agreed that the only answer was to call Dr. Rocco Carlone, the Chief, for a third opinion and abide by it.

Herb was insistent that we bring him in cold—tell him nothing about either of our conclusions so he wouldn't be influenced in his diagnosis and decisions. So, we called him—or—I should say, I called him—but with reservations. To be sure I'd not counter him by my tone or inflection, Herb stood at my side at the phone.

"Rocco, could you come right down to the Center? Herb Boyer and I have a complicated problem down here and we need your help."

"What's it all about? Is it a surgical case?"

"I don't know, Rocco, but it is urgent.

"What's the big mystery? Can't you at least clue me in?"

"Rocco, please, don't ask questions. This is a very peculiar situation. Just come."

We knew it wouldn't take long. With Rocco nothing ever does. And yet, the short wait became long minutes full of dire thoughts that seemed to compound themselves. How many times had I, as a physician, lived through such a drama with mounting tensions of an apprehensive family— hollow eyed—dry mouthed—shifting nervously from chair to chair, trying to distract one another with snippets of trivia totally unrelated to the crisis at hand.

When Rocco arrived, his cheery hello was melted by the heat of our serious mien. After introducing him to the family, we three adjourned to an empty conference room. In deference to my colleague, I chose my words very carefully.

"Rocco, we are dealing with a very serious and a very complicated problem. Herb and I cannot agree on a diagnosis and we desperately need your opinion. We've decided, in this unusual situation, that you not be swayed by our impressions until you have reached your own conclusion. Now, Herb, give him the history."

Boyer retold the whole story, pretty much as it would read in a text book, and then answered whatever additional questions Carlone had.

I watched Carlone very carefully through this whole recitation, wondering how he would react. Years ago he had been my mentor and I guess my awe and his aura would never rub off. He would always be my "Chief."

He was staring at the ceiling like he was searching out microscopic fly specks, but his mind was obviously racing as he let Herb talk without interruption. When he had finished, Rocco's eyes came down and then he impatiently said, "Let's go."

We marched back into the patient's room. Rocco asked a few more simple questions before he drew back the bed cover and proceeded with his quick, subtle palpation of the abdomen. When his fingers had answered all his doubts, he replaced the sheets, murmured a reassuring word to the patient, and we all marched back to the conference room.

"Well," I asked, "What do you think?"

"Well," he drawled as an echo to my words, "First off, there's no question this man has an acutely inflamed abdomen and he is plenty sick. So much for the obvious. Now, there are lots of things to consider. He is 73 years old and at that age he could have a cancer of the bowel and, although it's rare, it could perforate and cause peritonitis. This would produce this kind of picture."

"Once in a while," he went on, "a Meckel's diverticulum could rupture or even a carcinoid might develop an infection like this."

He was looking from Boyer's face to mine, apparently trying to catch a clue and then went on.

"I remember a case I had exactly like this one some years ago. He was one of those guys who used to chew toothpicks—always had one in his mouth. One day he came up with an acute abdomen and when I operated what do you think I found? A toothpick that he'd swallowed. It had burrowed its way through the wall of the cecum and gave him peritonitis. Almost killed him."

This sure wasn't the quick, confident Carlone I knew so well. This giant, this hero of mine, was rambling and meandering through the vaguest of diagnostic possibilities—cataloguing the fleas and overlooking the dog. I couldn't stand it any longer.

"Rocco," I begged, "What the hell are you talking about? What is this crap about toothpicks? For heaven's sake, stop talking nonsense and tell us what you really think is wrong with this man."

Suddenly, Rocco Carlone was himself again. My words seemed to have yanked him out of a bad dream. He jumped to his feet and with the clipped phrases of his usual racing speech, he practically shouted, "You want to know what I really think? I'll tell you what I really think. I think this guy's got himself a red hot gall bladder and we'd better damned sure crack him before it busts."

The elastic in me gave and I could feel the tension leave my back.

"Why the hell didn't you say so?", I snapped.

"Why? why?", he asked, "Because you guys paint me into a corner. You tell me you've got a cockeyed case—it's so unusual that you two geniuses can't get together on it. What

21

did you expect me to think? I say to myself—what are they pulling on me? This has gotta be something really rare. If it's a cock-eyed case, I gotta come up with a cock-eyed diagnosis. As far as I can see, it's just a cock-eyed gall bladder and we'd better get going. Let me call surgery. They should be ready in about 45 minutes."

Yes, it was a gangrenous gall bladder and yes, the patient did do well. And let it be told that some years later, when they honored him with a big formal dinner on the occasion of his announced retirement—to his chagrined amusement—he was introduced as the eminent, Dr. Rocco "Toothpicks" Carlone.

3

The Black and White of It

Some of his associates remember Dr. Rocco Carlone, the former Chief of Surgery of our Medical Center, for his prowess as a flawless operator; others for his colorful teaching rounds. But there are some who say his greatest claim to fame was bringing Simmie Sims into our Center family.

The Sims affair was purely fortuitous. Carlone was one of a dozen surgeons chosen from all over the country for a two-week stint of an exchange of knowledge and experience between American physicians and their European counterparts. It was sponsored by the International Surgical Society with the end hope of initiating an ongoing program of reciprocity and good will.

As the tour wore down, so did Carlone's old bones. The ordeal of performing against jet-lag for endless hours and then trying to sleep on strange beds took its toll. He'd had it with the gray chicken dinners, the pontifical banquet speeches and the endless too-often boring lectures. There was also the frustration of watching poor techniques performed in grossly inferior facilities. He counted the hours until he could return to the snuggle of his wife, the feel of his family, and even to the pressures of his patients.

Sitting with his colleagues in a tier of a rather shabby surgical amphitheater, his eyes drooping in fatigue, he barely heard an interpreter giving the current case history in stumbling English—"a strangulated hernia with signs of intestinal obstruction and tissue necrosis." The patient was wheeled in, quickly anesthetized, draped, and the operation began. After a first courteous glance of attention, something caught his eyes and popped them wide open. To an old hand like Carlone this kind of operation was no great shucks, but now he was seeing something unique. For the first time in the whole tour he was spellbound by the young surgeon—so adept, so punctuated and so graceful with every move and maneuver. With one hand he was holding the sick gut like a mother cradling her infant, and with the other, simultaneously, he was vigorously sewing, cutting and stitching. Carlone could only see his eyes between the mask and the surgical cap, but this had to be a young kid, but a kid with class.

While everyone moved on to a lecture room, Carlone stayed behind, riveted to the performance of the young man as he did another case and then another. Carlone knew. He knew that if it were at all possible, he wanted him at his Medical Center. He had never seen so beautiful a ballet of surgical expression in the hands of a relative novice. The cry in the old pro begged to clutch him under his wing—to teach him judgement, surgical knowhow, the when and how to accept a challenge at the bedside or in the operating room and the signals for retreat. He had to have him.

This was Friday, two days before the tour was to end at the Vilnius University Medical Center. Carlone wound his way to the surgical dressing room and introduced himself to Dr. Simcha Simmelowicz, who identified himself as Senior Surgical Fellow at the University Hospital.

On the spot Carlone offered him a corresponding fellowship at our Medical Center with the assurance that the financial details and visa requirements could all be worked out. The doctor's Polish widespread eyes brightened in disbelief, though—with his limited English—he just wasn't sure he had understood the proposition. It was only after an interpreter fully explained away all his doubts that—without a moment's hesitation—his smile and his eyes gave the answer. Of course he'd come. America—a big city—the big time in his profession. He couldn't believe it and he couldn't refuse it. He shook Carlone's hand and the pact was sealed. A release from the Vilnius University would be necessary and there would be a contract to sign. Carlone also made it clear that he would have to take a crash course in English during the three month interim while arrangements were being completed. With all this understood, the two parted with another hearty handshake, both of them convinced that their marriage had been made in heaven.

Carlone returned to a round of intensive meetings involving the top brass of the Center over the stance they would have to take on the newly formed Specialty Boards. He was adamant about going along with the required certification for operating privileges in order to retain the Center's status as a top teaching hospital. Between those meetings and his private practice, he stole the time to implement the final instructions, contracts and air tickets for his promising protege. Almost three months after Carlone had first seen him operate, Dr. Simcha Simmelowicz—with little baggage and lots of hope—appeared at the great entrance hall of the Medical Center.

One thing was immediately apparent. His English had become incredibly fluent, distinguished by only a taint of European accent. But something would have to be done about his name. How could the hospital personnel, patients, and particularly the paging operators ever be able to handle the "cha" and the "wicz" of their import? So—with Simcha's permission— the staff promptly rechristened him "Simmie Sims" and from then on, that's who he was.

So bright, so affable and so competent, he became a favorite of the interns, residents and visitants almost at sight. Dr. Meredith Lambert, ("Merrie" to the staff) our fifth year surgical resident, was assigned to be Simmie's special buddy— to squire him around and teach him the ropes. In short order, the two men graduated from buddies to deeply devoted friends. Between cases and in the quiet times of the evenings, they found so much to share—their ambitions, their values, their goals—whence they had come, and where they wanted to go. Each found in the other a bubbling source of freshness and a clean love of life. They were so different and yet so alike that they sometimes fantasized about a reincarnation from generations back that would make them true brothers under the skin. Was it just coincidence, they wondered, that a black American Baptist nicknamed "Merrie" became bound to a white Polish Jew named "Simcha", the Hebrew word for joy?

Simmie's first experience with the Center's shiny new instruments—the razor sharp scalpels, disposable syringes and catheters, and the endless supply of fresh towels and drapes was like a dream. He never could have imagined such an opulence of equipment. The surgical problems, however, were the same, so that he quickly adapted to his new American milieu, and became as effective and secure in our operating rooms as he was at Vilnius. Just as Carlone had recognized, he was a symphony of motion, performing the most difficult of procedures with the ease of an old pro. And, as Carlone had hoped, he developed the bedside poise and the keen judgment that marked him for greatness. He was a stimulus to the staff and an asset to the institution. Carlone, thrilled with his discovery of so precious a gem, was bloated with the pride of a new father.

As their friendship blossomed, Simmie was invited more and more often to Merrie's parents' home and welcomed more and more lovingly. When both men were off duty, there would be dinner and long evenings of conversation and discussion. Simmie was fascinated by the stories and folkways of the Lamberts that so paralleled the stream of black history in America.

Papa Lambert was a minister. Big boned, handsome and affable like his son, they could have been taken for brothers. Mama was a school teacher with enough of a residual drawl to specify her beginnings. They talked about roots, religions, the world around them and their concepts of the world to come. Friends and numberless relatives would drift in and out, freely adding their tuppence to the subject of the moment. It was a whole new arena for Simmie and he was an avid spectator.

One evening, after a delicious dinner, (which they always were to Simmie) Mama softly reminisced with the bits and pieces of what she could remember of her early years. "I never knew my father," she began, "but they told me he was a handsome young teenager, a happy-go-lucky laborer in a construction gang in our small town in Alabama. He was well-enough liked, except in the local white circles where he wao considered one of those 'uppity niggers'. He fell in love with Mathilda, the pretty little girl with dimples and pig-tails, who lived a piece down the dirt road. They were married long before they were twenty, and within the year, in their little mud floor shack by the light of a keroene lamp, I was born. There are times when I think about the primitive and putrid conditions under which some of us were brought into this world, I just can't believe how so many of us survived. It's really a miracle".

"I can't recall what my daddy was like, but I do remember there was always lots of singing and laughing in our little house. What there was to be happy about—I can't imagine. Maybe it was just lovin' each other so much. But that happiness didn't last very long." Mother Lambert choked up and stopped abruptly. The boys begged her to go on. She swallowed hard and struggled to get the words out. "One day they came and got him . . . Some paltry pieces of lumber had disappeared and someone pointed the finger at him . . . My mother never saw him again . . . They told her he had 'sassed' a guard in the jail and then tried to escape . . . The coffin came on a wagon . . . It was nailed shut . . . She watched them bury the box. Who or what was in it she'd never know. 'Please, dear Lord, let it be my man' was her only prayer, and . . . then and there . . she died with him. All the luster and life went out of her. She became a dullard, a working animal."

"Of course, slavery had ended long before, but the southern whites retained their tradition of 'care-taking' of their needy blacks. So—in that tradition—the family where mother had previously done day work, took us in—in exchange for the both of us working their fields and in their house."

"I remember like it was yesterday how I marched off to school every morning all scrubbed and starched. School was a dusty, stifling one room shack, but I loved being there. It was the only place I felt I could really grow. When I got home in the afternoon, I'd plant and pick in the fields alongside mother. There were times I was sure my back would break and I'd never be able to stand up straight again, but I didn't dare complain. Mother wouldn't hear me if I did. She was always silent and sullen. So you see, that's why the classroom—dingy as it was—was my only refuge from loneliness and hard work and just being poor, and I lapped up every morsel of learning I could grab there."

"My white family *did* encourage me to go to high school and, when I did well, on to the State University. I existed on the few dollars Mother could scrounge up. She would slip the money in my hand without a word, never asking about my studies, my friends, where I had been or where I was going."

"Then—one day in the spring of my senior year—there was an envelope from 'the family'. Inside was my mother's death certificate—'died of natural causes' with a one line personal note. They were sorry about her death, and, there was no estate. I couldn't believe it. She had never been ill—never missed a day's work. The worst of it was that I'd never know how it all happened. From the day Dad disappeared, Mother and I never really had any relationship. Yet I knew she was always there for me. Now, one bitty scrap of paper made me an orphan. The word was so cold and so frightening. For awhile I was plain numb, and then I burst. I don't know how long I just sat on a campus bench sobbing my heart out."

"And that's where I came into the picture," interrupted Mr. Lambert. "I was walking to a class when I heard that terrible sobbing. At first I couldn't tell where it was coming from, and then I spotted this pathetic little girl, curled up on a bench deep in the shadows of an old elm tree, drenched in the flood of her own tears. I don't know what made me sit down beside her, but that's what I did. I lifted her chin, and—oh my—was she pretty! Even with swollen eyes and the red running nose, she sure was something to look at!"

"Oh Emmanuel!" Mrs. Lambert broke in with the coy look and voice of a young girl. "Now you just let me finish. It really was like in the story books with Prince Charming appearing—like out of thin air—or as though the Great Reader up in his heaven took mercy on me and, with the flip of a page, started me on a new chapter. Anyway, Emmanuel let me talk and talk and talk away my heartbreak. He just listened and held on to my hand gently but very tight—and children I have to tell you, he's never let it go."

"Now I had something to strive for and someone to live for. While Emmanuel went on through Divinity School, I finished my teacher's degree and then together, we went on to marriage. And then Meredith came—what a wonderful day that was—the day he was born."

Merrie never tired of listening to the parts of his mother's bio—especially about the joy of his birth—and Simmie was completely enthralled. He had never even seen a black before he came to the States, much less know anything about them, and now he thirsted to know more.

Another time—a few weeks later—when the boys' off duty time coincided, Simmie coaxed the Reverand into telling his story.

"I sure had it better than Mama," he started. "My father was kind of an average black for his day. He was a Pullman porter in the Chessie system—well-liked and usually well-tipped. He loved the life he lived. He loved his kids, he loved his job, and he loved being married to Lessie."

"My mother, Lessie Lambert, was a powerhouse. She was the mainspring, the drive, the ambition of the brood. She made the laws of the house, policed them—and I can tell you—we kids didn't dare break them. Mama was rock solid. She was the BOSS!"

"Amen to that," Merrie's mother chirped in. "It took me years not to be scared of her. . . . but go on, Emmanuel."

"I sure do remember those years, darlin', but you gotta admit that Mama did have a soft side. She was always there for a hug, a little tender encouragement and lots of caring advice. Dad was off on the road so much of the time, it was really Mama who kept us loved up—all eleven of us. As soon as the oldest of us kids was about 5, we would have to take care of the 'new baby' so Mama could go off to her housework job. There was no lapse in her routine; bear a child, go back to work, bear a child, go back to work. After number 11, she quit breeding, but not working."

"As each of us grew into our teens, we were sent out to do all manner of odd jobs after school to bring in a few pennies. No matter what we earned, the rule of the house was that 10% had to go to the 'school fund', the holy of holies. That money was sacrosanct. It was banked regularly and no emergency could claim it. It could only be drawn for educational expense—tuition or books. Mother lived by the dogma that education was the ladder to success and she was zealous in helping us on the climb. This was the value system I grew up with, and it must have been a good one if a Pullman porter and a domestic could produce three school teachers, three attorneys, three government workers, a doctor and me, a minister—the lucky seventh out of eleven."

"A short time after I was ordained, Dad had a stroke and 'passed'. Mother Lessie accepted his death as a directive from above and took it like a major. She held tight her reins of the roost and she never quit working until her 65th birthday, and then, only when we ganged up on her and laid down the law. She still sits proudly on her throne like a queen with her thirty-four grandchildren added to her realm. She can't possibly remember all of their names, so the kids—when they visit her—have learned to present themselves with, 'Great Grandma, my name is (whatever), my mommy and daddy are (whoever)' To finish my story, Simmie, I have to tell you, that in our family, education is still the number one goal. It is still underwritten by 'The Lambert Fund', and it is still maintained by contributions from each working member of the family."

There were other times at the Lamberts' home when the minister or his wife or friends who had dropped by, would

exchange very disturbing tales of their past, tales pock-
marked by the slurs and bruises and cupidity they had suffered while they were trying to swim against the strong and
unebbing tide of a white society.

Simcha was spellbound by every word of every narrative.
He was fascinated by some of them, nodding in accord; vis-
ibly pained by others, swallowing repeatedly in empathy.
The Lamberts seemed to read his reactions, sense his kin-
ship and, in time, they began pressing him to talk about *his*
family and *his* past. As closely identified as he felt, he wasn't
yet ready to share the devastating memories of the desecra-
tion of his people. He would dodge a bit and detour a lot
into territory he could handle with some comfort. "You
want to know what kind of a kid I was? I'll tell you. I was
what you Americans call a bookworm. I loved learning. To
me it was like bursting through golden doors into endless
rooms full of exciting new facts and ideas. After studying in
school all day and finishing my chores in the house, I would
sit at my father's feet in the evening and beg him to teach me
all he knew of the Bible, the true meaning of the commandments and the essence of man's humanity to man. All of that
I learned at home. In the street world of kids—especially
the non-Jewish kids—I learned cruelty. In school they made
my life miserable because I was bright and because I was a
Jew. After school—only because I was a better athlete than
most—it was a different story. Then I was one of the guys.
They were happy enough to choose me for their team."

"Your English is amazing, Simmie," his friend Merrie
broke in. "You just couldn't have leaned to speak this well in
the short time you've been in the States. How did you do it?"

"You're right. Actually, Russian and Lithuanian were the
official languages we were taught in school. On my own, I
picked up a smattering of English and German through the
years. But when I took the crash course Dr. Carlone advised
before I came here, perfecting my English became my priority and I really gave it my all. Interestingly enough, in our
home my father insisted that we speak no language other
than Yiddish."

"Now what is Yiddish?" Mother Lambert wanted to know.

"Yiddish," he answered, "is a bastard mix of German and ethnic colloquialisms that, through the generations, have become staples in the vocabulary of European Jews."

The mention of Yiddish brought a snort of laughter from Merrie. He had to break in to tell the family how bizarre and hilarious it was to assist a surgeon who—in the taut concentration of an operation—would relapse into Yiddish expressions—how it would become kind of contagious.

"Can you imagine me," laughed Merrie, "the son of a Baptist minister, screaming 'oy vey' when something goes wrong in the operating room? Well, I have—many times. My good friend here usually calls his assisting intern or resident—male or female—'Boychick', and that's supposed to mean little boy. The assisting scrub nurse answers to 'Schickselah', the Yiddish term for a female gentile. He even gives orders during surgery in the same vernacular like, 'Come on Schickselah, are you asleep? This shamus is bleeding his life away. Give me a hemostat—another—another—schnell!' It's all done in affection, and in reciprocal affection, we rib and mimic him."

The Lamberts had a good laugh over their son's imitation and then asked Simmie what had motivated him to go into medicine and how and why he had wound up in surgery. Simmie explained that he had stuck his inquisitive fingers into every pie of learning and then one day had come up with the plum. It was the study of life and the mechanics of the human machinery that tantalized him the most and what propelled him to medical school. By his second year there, he knew that the vagaries of disease and inconsistencies of symptom diagnosis, draped and shaded with emotional overlay, were too haphazard for him.

Surgery—where one could define, excise, repair and thereby cure—that was what enticed him and what would be his career.

That answered, the Lamberts asked about his family and his life as a youth in Poland. Here Simmie clammed up. There were doors to his memory that he couldn't or wouldn't unlock. Impolite as it was, he had to leave. He had to get out into fresh air. He had to be alone.

He walked the long blocks back to the hospital trying to erase the nightmares the Lamberts' questions revived. He'd try to get a good night's sleep. He'd feel better in the morning. One always does.

Just as he started to undress he got a triple page, an urgent call to the emergency room. When he got there, he was led through a covey of personnel scurrying around the table in room #3. The resident straightened up and hurried his report. "I'm sorry I bothered you, Dr. Sims. I'm afraid it's too late to do anything anymore for this man. When they brought him in, judging from his obvious external wounds and widely dilated pupils, he must have been pummeled pretty badly. He was practically dead on arrival and at this point, he is totally unresponsive. He's gasping his last few breaths and there's no return in starting any resuscitative efforts on a guy with no brain."

On the table lay an elderly bearded orthodox Jew, wrapped in his cloak-like prayer shawl—the blue stripes and trailing fringes now spattered with blood. His face had been battered to a pulp—lacerated and black and blue. His grey curly beard was matted and sticky with the jelly-like clots. A glance at the cardiac monitor showed a flat line—his breathing had stopped—he was indeed very dead.

To answer his questioning look, the triage nurse told Simmie what the ambulance crew had reported. The patient was apparently reciting his evening prayers when he had been suddenly attacked by a couple of young hoodlums who had broken into the house and demanded money. Evidently the poor old man was too startled to respond so they just beat him savagely with some kind of blunt instruments, and when he fell to the floor, they raked his pockets and fled to the street. People heard the racket, saw the fleeing pair, called the police and the ambulance brought him in.

Simmie listened . . . but he didn't seem to hear. He was staring at the old man . . . but he wasn't really seeing him. After some long moments, he bent over slowly, cupped the

battered head in his hands and pressed his lips to the fore-
head with loving tenderness. As he straightened up, he
started to weep, silently at first and then with ever increasing wrenching sobs. He was way off in another world—con-
vulsing in an agony of his own. Suddenly, his eyes refocused
and when he became aware of the dumbfounded stares of
the attending staff, he jumped and bounded off like a frightened animal.

The next morning, Simmie was Simmie: quiet, affable, ef-
ficient, effective. But—something had happened that night.

Several evenings later, at the Lambert home, there were
things that were said that touched Simmie very deeply. It
was as if the dam that he had kept bolted so tightly suddenly
burst open. He started to talk, first in little spurts and then
in floods. He poured out his soul like never before and the
Lamberts listened for hours and hours—in awe, in disbelief,
in the utmost compassion.

At first there was no sequence to his reveries. The earliest
memories were of a vague and dreamlike shadowy existence—of living in a dappled forest that was cool and damp
and dark. He remembered sleeping on a bed of leaves and
clamboring about with an assorted gamut of ragged little
boys and girls. Phantom-like people glided in and out of the
forest shadows. The older women looked after the children,
teaching them how to clean themselves, how to tend their
tattered clothes, and assigning them little jobs picking ber-
ries, collecting twigs for small cooking fires, or lugging pails
of water from the stream that ran below. When he was left
alone, Simcha recalled sitting on a log amusing himself by
making endless changing shadows with the play of his fingers in the shafts of yellow light that sifted through the
branches high above. All the little ones were constantly reminded not to ever speak in a loud voice, or ever laugh or
cry. They were imprisoned in a hushed world that blended
into the quiet murmuring of the rustling leaves. The people
and the details were all a blur. Only the tone of his life was
the resounding memory—a resounding memory of a whis-

pered existence. Time was an unpunctuated procession between the darkness of night and the deep shadows of day.

As Simmie tried to replay this interval of his childhood, he became totally disconnected from time, place and his rapt circle of new friends. He was jolted back to reality with Merrie's interruption. "I don't understand why you were hiding in the woods. Did you run away from home?"

"Maybe I should explain it better and start at the beginning. My family lived in a small town about 20 kilometers from what is now Vilnius. Through many generations the village had developed into the hub for a group of small outlying farms. Produce would be gathered and brought to the town square where it was bartered locally or sold to dealers who had come from the city. There was an enclave of Jewish families who traded their goods in the general market, but they were confined to a few blocks and had to live inside their restricted little pale. Although they weren't permitted a synagogue, they did maintain a kosher butcher and observed, as best they could, the Sabbath and the Jewish holidays. My father was the village butcher and he doubled as the town mohel."

This time it was Mrs. Lambert who broke in. "Excuse me, Simmie, but you'll have to tell me what a mohel is."

"He's the man who performs the circumcisions that are ritual for every Jewish boy shortly after birth. That procedure, as you may guess, takes a certain amount of skill and sometimes I think I inherited his dexterity with the knife. Could you call that surgical roots? Incidentally, my father was also the titular Rebbe—the spiritual and religious leader of this small congregation."

Simmie went on, telling how hard a life it was for the Jews of their town. They were struggling farmers—breaking their backs day after day, fighting the unyielding soil and the mocking elements. And in the village they had neither voice nor weight. In addition to land taxes, they were burdened with a special "Jew Tax" for the privilege of being tolerated as alien guests of the state. They were allotted the worst stalls in the trading square and were bullied and bedeviled at the slightest provocation. Their philosophy for survival was, "It could always be worse." Resigned to their lot, they just shrugged and carried on helplessly—yet always under the oppressive and constant fear of physical hurt. Christmas and Easter were their most plaguing nightmares. That's when the drinking in town got out of hand and the holiday diversion was to "rough up the Yids". All too often roving bands of roistering soldiers would come barrelling through town and, in their unbridled violence, leave a trail of blood—a maimed or dead mother, father or child. There was no redress for the victims. They could only tend their wounded or bury their dead.

Simcha told the story as he had heard it about his father's father who had preceded him as the kosher butcher, the mohel and the Rebbe of the village. "My grandfather had been crippled as a young man and walked with a decided limp. How did that happen?" Simcha answered his own question. "Forced army conscription for all young men was the law of the land in many European countries. The Jewish recruits were invariably assigned the most dangerous posts and the most onerous duties. Rarely did any of them ever return either alive or in one piece. Parents learned fast that there were certain physical defects that could defer one from service, and that's when the 'specialist' became their saviour. He would travel village to village plying his life-saving trade on the 12 and 13 year-old boys. They would be gathered in the dark of the night to be 'treated'. It could be a sharp jab of the thumb in exactly the right spot in the groin to produce a permanent rupture. Or it could be a sudden deft hyperextension and torsion of the knee, enough to crack the joint, leaving the boy with a permanent limp. The 'specialists' knew all the regulations and, were not only expert in their crippling maneuvers that defeated the draft, but also in avoiding suspicion in their operations. And that's how my grandfather got his limp."

Simmie stopped short in his narration, gulped and wiped a tear. He then went on to tell how one evening his Grandpa was on his way home from market carrying a live chicken in each hand, when he lost his hat to a sudden gust of wind. As it rolled away, he chased it down a long, unfamiliar alley. Finally he reached it and was about to pick it up when he found himself surrounded by a group of teenagers in the middle of a game of stickball. Wildly excited, they abandoned their ball for the more thrilling game of hitting this defenseless little man with their sticks. They grabbed his hat, tossed it from one to the other while they kept clubbing him and pushing him faster and faster within their tightening little circle. "Dance, Jew, dance." "Dance, Jew, dance", they taunted him with their singsong. The poor old man hobbled painfully around that spinning, sickening little sphere, grasping desperately for his hat and panting desperately for breath. Groaning and bloodied, he finally clutched his hat, set it on his head and crumpled to the ground. A couple of men walking nearby were attracted by the racket, broke up the fiendish frolic and sent the kids running. They hoisted Grandpa by his armpits, literally dragged him the few blocks to the street where they knew the Jews lived, draped him across the handle of the courtyard pump and there they left him. By the time he was found by his neighbors, his life had fluttered out. He didn't have to die. He only wanted to get his hat. Didn't they know that a Jew feels that he lives his entire life in the presence of his Maker and in respect for Him, his head must always be covered?

Simmie paused, blinked away another tear, and then went on. "Merrie, I'm sure you've been told what happened the other night in the emergency room and I've never tried to explain it to you. Now perhaps you can understand. When I looked down at that dying man, I didn't see a stranger. Although I'd never met him, I just knew he was my own grandfather—battered and broken. We—you and I—work so hard to save a life, why should we lose so precious a one so easily, so casually, so unreasonably? We are taught to respect living tissue, to avoid damage to each and every cell, to handle membranes like filigreed lace. That is our surgical credo. What I saw on that table was a brain—the delicate repository of loving memory and lore—callously bludgeoned into a bloody, lifeless pulp. And in the haze around him, I saw grinning, prancing barbarians smashing statuary, crushing violins and burning books; Nazis pounding the hands of practiced musicians. I could hear the echoes of screaming torture. The bullies of the world, through the ages, were all in front of me, brutalizing innocent people for all kinds of reasons; for gold, religion, women, color, or just out of rabid hatred. It all got so real—so oppressive, I just couldn't bear it."

Simmie was drained.

A few of the Lambert nieces and nephews had wandered in to visit and had silently joined the spellbound audience. Little gasps slipped out with their handkerchiefs.

"Doctor," spunky little Sarah broke the tension, "what did they do to the boys who hurt your grandpa? Were they ever punished?"

"Nothing. Nothing could be done. Our people wept their burning tears and sadly buried their dead. Are you folks able to punish anyone when the Kluxers kill one of yours?"

There were no answers. The room got very quiet for a few uncomfortable minutes until Merrie asked, "Simmie, what happened to the rest of your family?"

"Well, after my grandfather's death, my father inherited the positions for which he'd been groomed almost from the time he could first walk—kosher butcher, chief mohel, and Rebbe to his little group."

"I haven't told you anything about my mother, have I? Her name was Leah Gruenberg. She was a pupil in my father's Bible class. For months she had been just one of the kids sitting at his feet, soaking up his every word. One day, quite suddenly, he noticed that this one little kid seemed to have blossomed overnight—and—in just the right places. She had become a lovely young woman and most exciting. Now *he* was the one who was adoring, and in a short time he matriculated his devoted student to a devoted wife. It was only a few months after their wedding that the big meeting was called."

"Every male was notified and every male came. There was reliable word that the Germans had started a war and were attacking and overrunning all the Russian fronts. Our Jews knew only too well that it would be a matter of days before Hitler's dreaded Nazis could be on their doorsteps and that their future or lack of it would be in their hands. Something would have to be done quickly. Everyone who had anything to say was heard and when the options were eliminated down to three, each was detailed and debated."

"The first course was to do what a group from a nearby town had done a year before—pack up whatever of their belongings they could carry and get out fast. Word came back that they had trudged their way clear across Europe, through Asia, and finally found a safe haven in China. A second possibility was suggested by a man who was home on leave from his government job as a Game Warden and Forest Ranger. He graphically described vast preserves of unexplored forest land far up north at the edge of the Latvian border. With no roads and no trails, only skilled woodsmen like himself could safely and secretly navigate the terrain. There, he said, they could nestle in and live for years—if that were to prove necessary. A third choice was proposed by one of the tired and timid villagers who couldn't conceive of the Germans ever reaching their anonymous little town, and if they did, he was certain it would be the Lord's will and therefore, the good Lord would surely save them."

At this point the Lamberts were literally on the edge of their chairs with no idea of how Simmie's drama would unfold. And Simmie was so sapped of emotion that he went on in an uninvolved third person style, telling them how the desperate little group discussed the positives and negatives all through the night. Finally, as the first of dawn's light sifted in, the decisions were made. Realizing that with the whole of Europe now at war, crossing the continent would be well nigh impossible, an attempt to escape to China was scrapped. Almost half of the villagers were fearful of leaving and opted to stay and pray. The other half decided to stake their fate on their neighbor, the Ranger, but only after he convinced them that he could indeed safely escort them to a totally secluded world where they could be hidden and survive. With plans formulated, they went back to their homes—some to stay—the others to pack for the road. Simmie's father was one of those who chose to leave while his mother's family chose to remain.

"By first nightfall, the determined little band was off." Simmie continued, "They travelled only in the dark of night and tried to rest out of sight during the day. Always avoiding the highways, they were led through small dirt roads and local lanes. Whenever they were stopped by inquiring strangers, they were coached to pass themselves off as itinerant workers on their way to a job. The trek seemed endless. Exhausted, tattered and always frightened, they began to wish they had never left their little village. Only the Ranger's confidence prodded them on. After countless weeks of threading their way through minute alleys, of trudging deeper and deeper under taller and taller trees, they finally reached their promised land—a spot where all the paths had long been gone."

The saga went on—how they settled into their hiding place, how they set up a haphazard kind of housekeeping and a cooperative division of labor. Somehow they weathered the frigid winters, the insect-ridden summers, the year round predatory animals—all of it compounded by constant hunger and fear.

It was early in their tortured march that Simmie's mother realized she was pregnant. The normal apprehension and discomfort of the first pregnancy was only exacerbated by the lack of privacy and other deprivations of the primitive life she had to endure. But Nature has a way all its own, and—in the dappled light of the forest, attended by the willing but untrained hands of a teenager—Leah gave birth to a rosy, healthy unblemished infant boy.

In this ragged little group's tense and hazardous struggle to survive, there was little to celebrate and yet, the arrival of that new life seemed to signal a flag of hope—a break in the grim sameness of every page of their calendars. And so it was that the new-born was named "Simcha", the Hebrew for joy.

In time—almost four years' time—the word came back through the Ranger that the war had ended. The Germans, he told them, had been routed out of their land and at last, they could go back—back to what—they wondered. All the way, as they passed burned-out farmhouses, gutted barns, seered fields and bombed cities, they could only pray that something would be left of their village and their homes. Their prayer was answered. It was a miracle. Nothing had changed. Weeds had grown between the cobblestones, the courtyard pump was crusted and hobbled with rust, but their houses were there, shuttered and locked as they had left them and with everything still in place. Later they learned that the townspeople, remembering back to the old superstitions about the Jews and the plague epidemic, had studiously avoided their little section in fear for their lives— certain that it was bewitched or at least, draped in a death-dealing miasma.

"But the people who stayed in the village were O.K. weren't they?" asked one of the Lambert children.

"No", Simmie answered. "Just a few days after my father's group started out for the forest, the SS Troopers had swooped into town, rounded up all the Jews who had stayed behind, threw them into trucks and carted them away like cattle to a slaughter house. Nobody ever saw or heard about any of them after that."

Simmie had been telling his story with relative calm, re-cycling the details that he'd heard over and over again. Now he choked up, paused for several seconds, swallowed hard and fought to release the words, "I can't remember my mother at all. She died when I was barely three. My father told me that there was no food fit for a baby and so when they were living in the woods, Mother just had to keep nursing me. Day by day she weakened and faded to skin and bones. I must have sucked her life away until one day, a siege of diarrhea wracked her feeble body and closed her eyes forever."

No one in the Lamberts' little sitting room moved. No one spoke. Only muffled sniffles and the rustling of tissues intruded on the deadly silence. Simmie was spent. He had buried the tragic story of his family and his people for years in an effort to fulfill the promise of his own life. And now that he had dredged it all up to consciousness, the catharsis was as agonizing as it was relieving.

Merrie couldn't bear the tension. "Anybody for a coke—a beer?" was the best he could come up with. It worked because everyone made it work. In no time the conversation mercifully veered to caffein, artificial sweeteners and assorted dietary fads and fancies.

But nobody who was there ever forgot that evening. The Lamberts, educated as they were, knew about the holocaust but had never identified one on one before. And, after sharing so poignant an intimacy, the friendship between Simmie and Merrie grew even stronger and more precious. While they worked long hard hours and slept short ones, the year they residented together just seemed to wash away. Their youth and the exhilaration of the large and varied pool of surgical cases that flowed through the Center carried them through the fatigue. It was a feast and they gorged themselves, loving every bite. Like all house men in training, what they enjoyed most was the wondrous opportunity of finally putting the medicine that had been static in the print of their books into real production. They were working with real people and their real illness, and yet, not having to assume the ultimate responsibility—that always being the domain and burden of the attending physician.

And Dr. Carlone, whom they worshipped, was always there—teaching and guiding. On any new procedure he would have the boys observe, then assist, then solo, but always under his supervision. With a kind of paternal pride, he watched his fledglings grow into accomplished, finished performers.

Aside from perfecting their techniques, Simmie and Merrie were growing in their understanding of the emotions of illness and wellness, the vagaries of symptoms and the hazards of fear. They learned equanimity in the face of disaster and the sense of urgency when seconds became vital. They met people of status minus character and men of means minus worth. A panorama of personalities was constantly passing through the Medical Center—and Pinhos Mehta was one they would soon meet but wouldn't soon forget.

4

The Slave Trader

The fifth floor of the Medical Center's new building was appropriately referred to as "The Gold Coast". All the rooms were private, and there were several luxuriously equipped corner suites, affordable to those who could pay the extra tab out-of-pocket. On this particular morning, Mrs. Cranston, the nurse assigned to the Gold Coast for the first time, was waiting outside of Suite #504 for instructions from Drs. Lambert and Sims, who were finishing their rounds on Dr. Carlone's surgical patients.

She couldn't understand why they were in the room so long. (On Sundays—with hospital services generally curtailed—doctors usually hurried through their rounds, anxious to get home to their families.) Since there was no obvious medical emergency, what could be the problem with that patient in 504? She couldn't resist leafing through the chart clipped to the door. The medical story she read was intriguing.

The patient, Pinhos Mehta, 42 years old, was from Curacao in the Netherland Antilles. At 18 he had suffered his first incident of bleeding from a duodenal ulcer, followed by recurrent episodes in the spring and fall of every year since. Treatment with antacids and diet would clear his symptoms each time, but with each change of the season—like clockwork—there would be another attack. Over the years the gnawing hunger pains became a part of his life. Lately, however, his symptom pattern had changed. The pain had become more persistent and was associated with nausea, loss of appetite and occasional vomiting. He was losing weight and vigor. It was more difficult to visualize his ulcer by x-ray. Yet the films did show scarring and barium retention in the stomach, indicating an obstruction at the pylorus. The consensus of the island's doctors was that his only option was surgery to cut out his ulcer and bypass the obstruction.

This resume of the patient's illness seemed creditable to Mrs. Cranston, but still left her puzzled as to how and why Mr. Mehta got from Curacao to our hospital in the States. That was later answered by the intern on the case who told her that the Curacao surgeon had heard Dr. Carlone speak at a conference in Miami the year before, and had been so impressed with him that he insisted he was the only man for the job.

And so it was that Pinhos Mehta, the owner of the "Little India Department Store" in the Otrabanda section of Willemstadt, accompanied by his wife and his three sons aged 12, 9 and 6 made the 3000 mile trip to our city. Because his medical records and request for "top accommodations" had preceded him, he was immediately admitted to Dr. Rocco Carlone's service while his family nested down in three rooms at the best available local motel. After a thorough review of his x-rays and lab studies, Mehta was taken to surgery for a subtotal gastric resection plus vagotomy. All went well. Now, 6 days after the operation, with the nasogastric tube removed, the abdominal wound was healing and he was started on a liquid diet.

On this Sunday morning, while the doctors were checking Mehta's vital signs, the family came bursting into the room for their daily visit. David, the youngest, ran to his father's bedside, tenderly kissed his cheek, and then whispered plaintively, "Papa, gits mir a Guilder. Ich bin sehr durshtig."

Simmie spun around, looked at the youngster, then at the father and started to laugh. He grabbed Lambert by the arm.

"Merrie, do you know what he said? That little guy told his father he was thirsty and needed a coin to buy a drink. Would you believe—he said it in Yiddish?"

Simmie turned to Mehta and asked, "Sind Sie ein Yid?"

"Of course, I thought you knew."

How could he have known? There had been no reason for Simmie to check the religious affiliation of his patient. In fact, when Simmie first saw him before surgery, his impression was of a short and squat young man with a tawny complexion, quite characteristic of the Portuguese and—although it was of no particular concern—probably Catholic. So, he was not only amazed that Mehta was Jewish, but that he spoke Yiddish, which he had firmly believed was fast becoming a dying tongue.

And—this was the distraction that had detained the doctors in #504 and had Mrs. Cranston tapping her toes in the hall.

Simmie asked Meredith to finish the rounds without him. Now and here—in the most unlikely place—he had struck a chord and he couldn't let go.

"You must be a new refugee to your island?" he said questioningly.

"No, my friend, my forebears arrived in Curacao almost 300 years ago. Through the centuries, with the ups and downs of commerce, some moved out to Brazil, Jamaica, Venezuela and Panama, but my family managed to stay."

"But why the Yiddish? Isn't Dutch the official language of the island?"

"Well yes, and then again, no. Dutch is now the official language in the schools, courts and government. However, at one time or another, Curacao has been owned by the French, the English, the Spanish and the Portuguese so there are remaining enclaves of all those former nationals, and to function socially and in business, we have to communicate with all of them. For that reason our children must learn five languages in school."

Simmie looked over at Abba, the eldest. It was hard for him to believe that that pubescent body harbored a brain that could accommodate all those languages.

"That's not all," Mehta continued, "We also speak a kind of patois called Papiamento that is indigenous to our island.

You could call it our street language. Actually, it's a concoction of Portuguese, the slang of the slave traders and the jargon of the slaves themselves. If you are not familiar with it, it makes absolutely no sense. In fact, the word 'papiamento' is Portuguese for gibberish or muttering. My children speak that too—especially with their friends."

"You mean, even the little ones? Hey, that makes six languages." Simmie was as floored by that as he was by Mehta's very literate command of English, which he apparently could have so little occasion to use.

While their father was talking, the kids were silently and politely nodding their heads in corroboration.

"But, how about the Yiddish?" Simmie asked.

"If a head is big enough for six languages", Mehta replied, "It can stretch for one more. Surrounded by so many cultures and diverse roots and religious beliefs on our little island, I have felt—like my fathers before me—that our children must be anchored to the solid ground of a heritage that is their own. In school and on the street, in their everyday communication, our boys use all of the languages they have learned, but in our home and between us, I insist that we speak only Yiddish. That—in addition to the children's extra-curricular religious school and our Temple affiliation is my way of insuring the security and permanence of my family's Judaism."

Simmie was struck as by a clap of thunder with the echo of "only Yiddish in the home". He stared at the man propped up on his pillows, but he didn't see Mehta. It was his own father he saw—and he heard him saying, "Only Yiddish in my home."

As much as he wanted to linger and learn more about these foreigners who had so strangely and suddenly become his kin, he had to finish rounds and write the orders for Monday's surgical schedule. He waved a quick goodbye, but he knew he'd be back.

That evening—at his almost routine Sunday dinner with the Lamberts—Simmie watched the little ones' eyes boggle when he told them about the Mehta children who, at their ages, could speak in 7 languages. A 12 year-old speak 7 languages? No way! Something wrong somewhere! He knew he could never make them believe it.

The pay-off came a few days later. Simmie had tried his school French and his home Yiddish with young Abba and there was no question of the boy's fluency and rich vocabulary. Yet he couldn't resist testing a mite further.

"Abba", he asked, "If you wanted a book for your own reading pleasure, which language would you choose?"

The boy's answer was a stunner. "That would depend on who wrote the book. If it were Van Paassen, I would want it in Dutch. If it were Moliere, I would get it in French. Certainly, I would have to read Shakespeare in English. Why should I lose the flavor of the original in someone else's translation?"

"That from a 12 year-old—incredible", Simmie mused.

The youngster fascinated him, but then, so did the rest of the family. Whenever he could snatch a few free moments from his busy schedule, Simmie would head to #504 to pump as much biography as he could out of Mehta, knowing that his impending discharge would inevitably end their close relationship. The family saga trickled out in these catch-as-catch can times, but ultimately it could all be pieced together. It began around 1649—and—on a gruesome note.

Pinhos Mehta's lines led back to Josef Metrovic, a farmer who plodded through day after day, tending his small parcel of land on the outskirts of a little Polish village. Like his fellow Jews, who were relegated to common labor and ineligible for the niceties of life, his only incentive was to keep food on his family's table. The world beyond his tedious routine was always far beyond him. So how could he believe the rampant rumors of a vast surge of pogroms sweeping his country—the horror stories of restless Tatars devastating cities and murdering thousands and thousands of innocents—most of them Jews?

Then it happened. One day while he was working his plot, he heard terrifying cries coming from the direction of his farmhouse. He raced over a little rise to see a group of

Cossacks raiding his hen house. Between swills of vodka and swells of drunken laughter they were kicking their heels in a kind of madman's dance. Some were chasing the hysterically squawking chickens to tie them up and carry them off for loot, and some were scrounging for eggs, collecting them in their hats.

Panic-struck, Josef tore through the door of his house and there—in the kitchen—was his baby hanging upside down from a hook, his head squashed into a pulp, the blood dripping into puddles on the floor. And just a foot away was his wife—motionless—with a Cossack officer heaving and grunting on top of her as he thrust in his brutal rape—completely oblivious to the wild intruder.

Josef rushed up behind him, raised his razor-sharp sickle high above his head and plunged it down with all his might. With one great shudder the heaving stopped, the grunting stopped, the beast's head dropped. Josef grabbed his arm and turned him over. He could see the point of his blade sticking out of a now blood-drenched shirt. He knew that the man's heart must have been torn wide open. Gently he pulled his wife's skirt down to cover her shame. Her head was twisted like a battered doll, her neck had been broken. She was dead.

Josef was wild with rage, crazed by fear. While the soldiers in the yard were impatiently calling their captain, he bolted through a back window, past the outhouse, through the trees and down the path to the road. He never wanted to see this stained and hideous land again. He set his heart and his head and his eyes toward the sea and his legs followed in the unrelenting jog of a wounded hound. After days that he couldn't track, he stumbled into a port, and—in the dark of night—crawled unnoticed into the hold of a ship being readied to sail. When his body, limp and semi-conscious, was dumped with a cargo of Ukrainian wheat out of the ship's hold into a retaining bin on the dock, he came to his senses. Luckily a stevedore, who was levelling off the grain with a large wooden paddle, spotted the bloodied body and called for help.

In no time a sizeable crowd gathered. They tried to shake him awake to question him, but he couldn't understand their foreign tongue. And they couldn't understand the strange croaking sounds that were the pleas of a parched and half-starved man for food and drink. They were about to call the police to have him jailed as a stowaway when a properly dressed young man elbowed his way to the front of the group. One look and he recognized Josef as one of his own by the cut of his hair. "Redst Yiddish? he asked.

Feebly Josef stammered, "Ja–ja–Ich red Yiddish." And these were the magical words that gave Josef open sesame to a new life of freedom in the City of Rotterdam.

About a hundred years earlier—when the Inquisition ordered all citizens of Spain and Portugal to adopt Catholicism or accept the stake—the Jews and the pseudo-convert Marranos who could afford it, fled to a haven in the Netherlands. There they were granted all the liberties of religion and citizenship. It wasn't long before they became a separate yet involved and contributing segment of their Dutch communities. The more enterprising found their niche in the burgeoning financial growth of the times. Propelled by the exciting potential of trade in the fast-opening panorama of the New World, some even invested heavily enough in the East India Company to become large and influential stockholders. That was the success story of the family of Josef's rescuer, Henrik Zieman.

Josef's success story began the day Henrik had him carried to the servants' quarters of the Zieman estate. There he was bathed and bedded, nourished, and slowly rehabilitated. When he was well enough, the elders in the group took him under their wing. They expedited the provision of proper identification papers; gave him the name of Jaacob Mehta; had his hair recut in the Dutch style. They welcomed him with their recognition, started him on manual labor around their various homes, and—until he could handle the Dutch language—Yiddish was their medium of communication.

Detailing his reminiscences apparently drained Mehta. His words stopped, his eyes closed, his head dropped back into his pillow. When the doctors started to tip-toe out of the room his eyes popped open. "No, no, don't go", he called them back. "I'm not tired. I was just wrapped in my thoughts. Actually—it's one recurring thought—that it was the Tsedakah of Hendrik and his family that was the salvation of Josef and my family. I'm sorry—I should explain 'Tsedakah' is the Hebrew for benevolence—concern for your fellow man, helping the less fortunate. It was in that Jewish tradition that the ragged and wounded young man who was fished out of the wheat bin became the beneficiary of the Zieman's caring custody.

After a deep sigh and now fully alert and composed, Mehta continued his saga. He went on to say that as soon as Jaacob could be trusted, he was put in charge of the Zieman's household affairs, the food ordering, the supervision of their servants. His next promotion was to a desk in the counting house of the business; keeping records and accounts of the position of their ships, their bills of lading and the monies exchanged. His diligence, in addition to an innate feel for commerce, rewarded him with increasing responsibilities each year and an insider role in the family's business.

One fateful day Jaacob was invited to a meeting of the company's governors. Their dealings with the Spanish 'asientos' in the Caribbean islands, particularly Curacao, had become the largest part of their overseas dealings and the most lucrative. Most of their ships were being used to transport slaves from African, Brazilian and Venezuelian ports via Curacao—making that island the logical hub—the staging area for this human cargo before shipment to the southern ports of the American colonies or to one of the other Caribbean islands. Having a trustworthy agent at their Curacao docks to handle the details of the shipments and the intricacies of the money exchange became essential. This job—along with a part interest in the profits—was offered to

Jaacob. Unencumbered by the family he was still mourning, he jumped at this chance of a new life and perhaps, his financial fortune.

With no stomach for sea travel, Jaacob spent most of the journey from Rotterdam in his bunk—miserable with mal de mer. When 'Land Ho' was finally called, he fell to his knees and fervently thanked the Lord for his survival. His business diaries recorded that—weak and debilitated as he was—when he walked down the gangplank and caught his first glimpse of this charming, chattering tropical wonderland, he was so exhilarated that he knew this would be the end of one of his lives and a reincarnation into a new and brighter one.

Jaacob was surprised to find a fairly large community of Jews already living on the island. Some had come to escape the oppression and tragic memories of their European homelands, and others were agents like himself who were sent by trading companies. And—there were always the adventurers searching for their Camelots in the New World.

He had no trouble making friends and establishing himself in his new environment. Business was thriving and he thrived along with it. The slave trade had become standardized. A ship's captain would sail to Africa with an order for so many thousand tons of slaves, and—figuring in an expected 25% loss due to death on the voyage—he could estimate his costs and his probable profits.

Curacao was where the action was; where the blacks were debarked, sorted and herded into holding pens; where they were fed, clothed and given minor medical care. And, after recovering from the rigors of their voyage, they were sold in parcels and separated for transport to their final destinations.

The prices were fixed too. A healthy young male (age 20–40) would go for X number of Guilders and lesser amounts could buy females, men with blemishes or disabilities like missing teeth, a blind eye or a withered limb. The Islanders waited at the auctions for the prime specimens to be sequestered and then bid for the leftover bargains. Some of these "sale" items were kept on the island to work in the homes of the native whites. After a period of years, many of them were granted their freedom or were able to buy it and that's what accounted for their eventual proliferation into a large free black community.

That it was the slave trade that kept the ships sailing and the gold flowing was of no more concern to Jaacob than it was to all the others who were so devoted to profiteering. Nor was he troubled by the long hours and hard work that went with his job. He was producing, advancing financially and his success helped dissipate the bitter memories and the excoriating dreams of the brutal massacre of his wife and child. He had a large house built for himself, and when he needed help to take care of it, the "bargain sale" was his resource. Amongst the leftovers he had spotted a pleasant enough looking black woman who was cowering in a corner of the group, holding firmly onto a little girl who looked as frightened and bewildered as her mother. Something in this tender picture touched Jaacob so deeply that he immediately chose them—even though it meant paying much more than he ever intended. Overnight, it seemed, the little girl who seemed so young when he bought her, blossomed into a beautiful young lady, and he found himself most attracted to her. She readily accepted his advances and the occasional invitations to his bed as one of her household chores, and soon—nursing a robust, very black baby boy—became just one more part of her job.

Jaacob, the child's owner and father (not an odd combination for the times) took him to the synagogue one day and had him pronounced a Jew. That was akin to the gift of a life insurance policy, Mehta explained, because as a Jew, according to a Biblical law, no matter what happened to his master, after six years of servitude the boy would automatically be granted his freedom.

Yoyo (that was his nickname) was a healthy, happy child and grew into a handsome and industrious young man. When he was old enough, he worked for Jaacob as a free man receiving a regular wage, and was always identified as

Mehta's son. He forfeited the name "Yoyo" for another, however, when he applied for a marriage license only because the clerk couldn't quite make it out. The closest he could come to "Yoyo", Mehta's son, was "Joe Mettison" and so it remained.

"To this day," Mehta continued, "There are hundreds of Mettisons on Curacao and all the islands around. There are Mettison teachers, lawyers, doctors and many in government service. Maybe it's chauvinistic, but I always enjoy thinking that it is their black skins parlayed with their Jewish brains that's made them such achievers. Although by strict definition, they're not really Jews, I consider them part of my clan, and everyone knows that at my Little India Department Store, a Mettison automatically gets a 10% family discount off any purchase."

Mehta started to chuckle. "By now, you must be wondering where I fit into all this. Well—I'm getting to that. When Jaacob was approaching sixty, he became concerned about perpetuating his lineage. In our Jewish writings, you see, one's seed is hallowed. Since there were no eligible Jewish women on the island, he put in his order (so to speak) with his company, and it was promptly filled. A very acceptable thirty-five year old widow was 'shipped' in from the Netherlands, and, as quickly as gestation permitted, she presented him with an heir, and that's how the Mehta name and line survived—Thank God."

One Saturday evening, when Pinhos Mehta was almost ready to be discharged from the hospital, he arranged for a sumptuous gourmet dinner to be served in his suite for his family, including Sims and Lambert, who had become his extended family. They discussed world affairs, local politics, the effects changing times had wrought on people and the ways they lived their lives. At a pause in the interplay of conversation, Merrie posed a very measured question—a question that had obviously been troubling him.

"Mr. Mehta, you told us about the slave trade in your land as casually as if it were the selling of yard goods or pounds of coffee. Did your people have no compunction about living off the sale of human flesh? Didn't they or you realize how you dehumanized your fellow man, what torment you subjected them to? You and your race who gave the world the Ten Commandments—how could you have broken them like pagans? And how do you seem to condone such bestialities—even now?"

Unblinking, unflinching, Mehta looked at Merrie with the indulgence of a parent trying to instruct his child. "I've been waiting for that question. I just wasn't sure when you'd ask it. Dr. Lambert, you must try to close your eyes to the present and open them to the culture and attitudes of that era. Remember that slavery had been indigenous to the life and economics of civilization from the first day of recorded time. Every form of society had it in one form or another—even the 'People of the Book'. Believe me—you can find rules and regulations governing the treatment of slaves in the Old Testament."

"Slavery had always been the accepted way of treating prisoners of war—were they soldiers or civilians. In the beginning the African chieftains conformed to that tradition, trading their prisoners of war for trinkets and baubles. But when the demand became greater than the supply of captives, and they were offered payment in monies of account, they fabricated their own prisoners of war by raiding neighboring villages and kidnaping what had become a precious human commodity. On our end, business was business, and we did wink at the so-called 'prisoners of war' we were buying and selling. There was plenty of evil in the whole system—I have to admit that."

"And yet there was some decency in our operation," Mehta explained. "Curacao was known to be the best of all the stations on the way—the place where slaves were treated relatively well. In fact, one Dutch officer wrote in his memoirs that 'the domestic slaves are better cared for in Curacao than many a maidservant in the Netherlands'. Of course— that doesn't whitewash the whole issue of how they were procured and the indignities they had to suffer before they were placed in their ultimate work. Curacao actually sanctioned slavery by law which made the practice of it an inalienable right of Protestants, Catholics and Jews alike. Even the synagogue, the famous Mikve Israel that is still standing, once owned a slave."

"Ultimately," Mehta went on, "and I tell you this—not to mitigate our guilt—but in time, all the island's religious groups, particularly the Quakers, began to question the abuses of the practice. And, long before your Lincoln's Emancipation Proclamation, Curacao declared all of its slaves free."

The young doctors didn't get a chance to rebut or argue their case. An urgent page from the emergency room cut off any further discussion and sent them flying down the hall.

A few days later—on the evening before his discharge—the team that had so devotedly pulled Mehta through his surgery—gathered in his room for the 'fond farewells'. "I've been wanting to ask you," Simmie broke into the emotional silence, "How come a nice guy like you got himself a peptic ulcer? That's usually the badge of an anguished soul."

"You forget, my friend, that I am a product of my genes. Old Jaacob Mehta, my genetic source, frequently mentioned the gnawing belly pains in his diaries, and what can you guess killed him?—a hemorrhage from his stomach. It's all in the records"

"And talking about genes, these last few days I've been overwhelmed by a feeling—almost an obsession—that when I leave here, I will be leaving more than friends behind—that the spirits of the three of us had to have touched somewhere before. Your forebears—the Simmelowicz clan and mine, the Meclovic clan, did live in the same Polish village at about the same time and could well have been brothers and sisters or uncles and aunts."

"And, Dr. Lambert, you know, that with all those thousands and thousands of blacks funneled through Curacao, that mother and child old Jaacob bought in the market may very well have been your ancestors. If so, Yoyo was a product of our combined germ plasm. Now can you see how the three of us—you, Merrie, and you Simmie and I must truly be blood brothers."

There was silence in the room and a deep sense of wonderment. How could anyone respond to that? After a few seconds, Mehta cleared the lump in his throat, took each of his doctor's hands, held on to them and—with an embracing look and puckish grin—said his 'goodbye'. "Good luck, my cousins. Please come visit us in Curacao some day soon. It will be my honor to be your host, and you'll have the bonus of using your family discount at my store."

The next morning Mehta was gone.

5

Cut Price

We were talking about a near miss in the operating room that afternoon. A vessel had slipped off a moderate sized artery and the blood began to spout. The patient's pressure dropped precipitously. He was sliding into shock. There was pandemonium. Fortunately, within minutes of frantic measures, the emergency was brought under control and "the sweat was off". That brush with catastrophe really shook us all up. Losing a life to an incurable disease is devastating enough. A death due to a preventable error is truly unconscionable.

This case was such a close call that it reminded me of one we had a while back where a surgeon goofed—at the expense of the patient—of course. But that time it was the surgeon who paid the most.

Bill Lucas was one of the old line surgeons at our Medical Center long before the days of specialty boards and quality control. At that time any medical graduate who wanted to specialize could apprentice to an established surgeon, work in his office for a year or more and then strike out for himself. Or—for a price—he could take a course at some European surgical clinic and come home with a gilded certificate anointing him a "Surgeon". Diplomas from either of these short-cut training programs were no affidavit of competence, and their recipients were not above mishaps in the operating room. If they were wise enough to profit from their errors of judgment or performance, they could get by, and in time, achieve some measure of success. Lucas was one of these. Although he was only adequate as an operator, he was a mogul at money-making and smart enough to be aware of his limitations. Why else would he have confined his practice to foreign neighborhoods, using the small suburban hospitals with limited staffs and more limited teaching programs? All that these institutions needed to stay above water was a steady flow of patients to fill their beds. The doctors were their providers so they could ill afford questioning their qualifications or ethical capacities.

To his ethnic flock, Lucas was God. In their trusting eyes he could do no wrong. His mind, his hands and his degree held the answer to all of their ills. Little did they suspect that many of their minor surgeries were too often performed on skimpy indication; that many an innocent uterus or appendix had been snatched for dubious gain to them, but for positive benefit to their surgeon.

And—Bill Lucas' business was strictly cash. His honest hard-working patients were not into charge accounts or insurance programs or second opinions. They confidently chose their doctor, followed his advice to the letter, and without question paid promptly in wrinkled dollars.

Lucas, however, was a rung above many of his confreres. He coveted his privileges at our Medical Center and— although it was almost always for an uncomplicated procedure like a simple hysterectomy—on occasion he did admit a patient there. Having his name on the operating schedule, sitting in on some of the lectures or being seen trailing along on grand rounds seemed enough to slake his thirst for professional status.

There were times though, when Lucas would cautiously stretch his limits. If a prominent member of his neighborhood clientele insisted on being operated at the Medical Center, and Lucas thought he could get away with it, he would do it himself. But if he foresaw any problem, he was judicious enough to refer the case to a surgeon whom even he acknowledged as more capable.

The case that resurfaced for me that afternoon was that of Stefan Pintar, the highly respected president of a local bank. He had had an attack of gallstone colic and was advised by his family doctor to have his gall bladder removed. He would have no other than his good friend, Bill Lucas, do the job, but—apprehensive about the facilities and after-care in the small community hospitals—he insisted on the Medical Center. Pintar was young, lean and healthy. Certain that this case would be a breeze, Lucas had him admitted to the Center and scheduled for the next morning.

When the abdomen was opened the first hint of trouble appeared. The gall bladder, instead of poking up into the incision, was tucked deep down, adherent to the undersurface of the liver. By the time Lucas dissected his way to the cystic duct, he found himself operating at the bottom of a pit. Suturing off the duct at the point where it runs into the common bile duct and tying off the associated artery and vein is usually simple. Doing the same maneuvers at the bottom of a well, however, demands experience and inordinate skill. Lucas was short on both. The vessels and ducts were so far down that they were beyond his grasp. Widening the incision didn't help so he kept fumbling away—unable to properly set his instruments, to position his ligatures or tie his knots. His hands were going limp. He began to perspire, to pant for air, to panic. Yet he knew he couldn't quit. Jamming his hand into the incision, he tried to force his way to reach the duct. In his rough groping, the tissues tore, blood and bile welled up around his hand. There was nothing he could do to stem the tide. He poked and he pushed, but to no avail. Seeing his patient's sterile drapes soaking in the red of his blood and the green of his bile, Lucas feared the worst— that he might have ruptured the liver. He blanched, his legs turned to rubber and the room began to spin. He knew that if he didn't get out of that operating room in a hurry, he would faint and fall to the floor. In a feeble croak the words came out: "Get somebody, get anybody, get help!"

As Lucas' hands dropped to his sides, the resident who had been trying to assist him packed the wound with gauze. The frantic circulating nurse dashed out into the hall in hopes of quickly finding another surgeon. She practically ran into Dr. Simmie Sims, who at that moment was on his way from one case to another. She grabbed his arm and—too frightened to talk or explain—pulled him to the nightmarish scene of Lucas, leaning across a flooded operating table, staring into space and babbling incoherently.

Reassured by the sheer presence of Simmie, the nurse, in breathless clipped phrases, tried to fill him in on their disaster: "Cystic duct is open. . . . no tie on the artery. . . . probably nicked the common duct. . . . lots of little bleeders. . . . pressure getting feeble. . . . no time to waste." With that, she took Lucas by the arm and led him out of the room.

Simmie had listened intently, scanned the anxious and troubled faces of the surgical team, and in seconds was out of the room and back in clean gown and gloves ready to do battle. Funnel-vision focussed on what had suddenly become his problem, he slowly removed the packing, plunged into the blood and bile filled incision, and—with one finger—blindly groped for the pulses and the feel of their patterns of flow.

"Boychick", he commanded, "Suck it out". And to the nurse, "Munyan—suture—another Munyan—another—another. Come on, Schwester, MOVE!" His hand was in the hole and he was clamping and sewing something on the bottom. His whole being with all its skill and cunning was in that cavity, mobilized to save a life. When his hand came out the blood had slowed, but the bile continued to well up and stain each fresh towel in its place.

"O.K. Boychick. Get a suction down to the bottom of that Gott verdampte crater and let me have a look at what we've got." Now he could see the untied end of the cystic duct. Again—with his hand curved in a beautiful arch—he was back in the incision sliding a suture over his finger, then around the duct, and tying it tightly shut, but the flow of bile continued to fill the hole.

"Schicksele, get me a 'T' tube. You're right, we've got a leak in the common duct. No problem. A couple of days of closed drainage and he should get along fine."

In a matter of minutes, the tube was deftly placed and the bile could be seen running down the long arm of the tube into a collecting bag instead of welling up and fouling the incision.

To the circulating nurse, "Schwester, fix the light and let's get another look."

The gloved hand went swiftly back into the hole, tied off the cystic vessels and ligated the remaining bleeders. Finally, it was dry. This had been like a sudden summer storm, Simmie thought. Now the winds and the rains had passed and the sun was shining again. He started to close the wound, leaving the 'T' tube sutured in place, and when they reached the superficial layers of the abdomen, he left it for the resident to finish. Only then did he permit himself to raise his head, straighten up, and take his gaze away from the operative site and walk out.

The resident just stood there; stunned, unable to believe what he had just seen. It all had happened so fast that he couldn't unravel the sequence. He did remember his own panic when he was unwittingly sucked into a partnership with Dr. Lucas' devilish dilemma. But how did Simmie take over and smoothly convert the harrowing ordeal into such an easy case? What an exhibition! He would never forget it.

The surgeon's lounge, as always, was disheveled with the litter of scattered newspapers, half drained coffee cups, discarded surgical caps and masks. Groups who had just finished or were waiting for their cases to come up, were huddled in clusters of conversation. Only Bill Lucas sat in a corner alone—still gowned and soiled with the blood and bile of his operation. His face was taut with agony. He neither heard nor saw anything around him. He just stared at an invisible spot on the floor—with Lord knows what on his mind. When Simmie walked in, he jumped up and dashed over to him. Simmie waved him off and—anticipating Lucas' thank you's—reassured him with the terse non-committal, "No sweat, Bill. Your patient is O.K. They're closing him now. We had to put in a 'T' tube and I ordered up a unit of blood, but he is O.K."

Lucas tracked Simmie into the dressing room, reached into his locker and pulled out a fist-full of bills. He grabbed his arm and swung him around to face him. "Simmie, you saved my life. I don't know why, but I began to feel so faint and sick that I just couldn't finish the case". Lucas held up his hands preparing to count out the money. "How much? I'll pay you anything you ask . . . you deserve to be paid . . . you really did the case . . . you saved my life."

"Bill, you seem to have forgotten that guy on the table. His was the life I saved—not yours. Forget it. I don't want your money."

Simmie pushed his hands away and turned to change into a clean scrub suit for his next operation. Lucas wouldn't be put off. Again he grabbed Simmie's arm and turned him around.

"Anything you ask. You have got to take it."

"Bill, put your money away. I don't want it. I won't take it. You owe me nothing. Whatever I did was for the patient—not you."

Lucas wouldn't let up with his badgering. He kept waving the hand full of money until Simmie, in obvious annoyance, looked him straight in the eye and challenged him; "Bill, you really want to do something—something worthwhile? I'll tell you what you can do. I want you to pledge ten thousand dollars—yes, ten thousand—to the United Black Fund. That will put a deserving black student through school. It could maybe help to heal your conscience too."

Lucas stiffened. Ten thousand? He was thinking of three or four hundred dollars as an ample (if not generous) reward, but ten thousand—and to a Negro fund. How could he ask me that? He started to demur, but when he realized that a couple of surgeons and surgical residents had walked in and became privy to the conversation, he was stymied.

All of them must have heard what had happened in Room #5 and now he was cornered. There was no way out. "O.K., Simmie, I'll do it. Just trust me. I'll take care of it."

But Simmie apparently didn't trust him to take care of it. He picked up a copy of the day's surgical schedule, turned it over and wrote on the blank side, "I, Dr. William Lucas hereby pledge the sum of ten thousand dollars to the United Black Fund, that sum to be paid within the year."

He handed it to Lucas and told him to repeat it aloud so that the others in the room would hear. With Simmie and two of the residents as witnesses, Lucas grimly signed without another word. Simmie carefully folded the sheet and slipped it into a pocket of the shirt hanging in his locker, turned the key in the steel door, pinned the key to his scrub suit and walked out to finish his surgical schedule.

When the room gradually emptied out, Lucas could feel the tension flowing out of his frame. He washed slowly and methodically and dressed back into his street clothes. When his necktie was properly knotted and his jacket back on, he moved to the mirror to pat his hair in place and smoothe his thin mustache to its prescribed contour. Last came the starched breast-pocket handkerchief that he fastidiously pleated in the four points of the current fashion. Then he stepped back for a full-length appraisal. Confident that he reflected the image of the successful doctor, he strutted down the hall to report to the family of Mr. Stefan Pintar.

There they all were, huddled in a corner of the surgical waiting room, nervously watching the door for the arrival and pronouncements of the Great God Lucas. And Lucas, playing that role as if he were to the deity born, breezily assured them that there was no problem. "Everything went as smooth as silk and he will do just fine. He's still coming out of his anesthetic, but you'll be able to see him in his room in about an hour."

Although Simmie never talked about "the case", the staff had no difficulty piecing all the details together from what the resident had told them plus a lot of loose talk from the two nurses who had been assisting. They had both been so shocked by their involvement in the potential tragedy that they talked about it—almost third person—excitedly and graphically as if they had been passengers in an almost total auto accident.

Lucas faithfully visited Pintar every day. The 'T' tube drained, and when the cholangiogram showed no residual stones, it was yanked without undue incident. The wound healed over and the patient went home. Soon he was back at the bank and would rave to anyone who would listen about what a fine surgeon his dear friend Bill Lucas was.

A year slipped by and Dr. Meredith Lambert was finishing his five year residency and getting ready to leave. He had accepted a head teaching position in the surgical section of a prominent Baptist hospital in the south. Simmie was winding down too, very anxious to get back to Vilnius to marry his technician girl friend, and then to explore the possibility of a permanent post in an Israeli hospital.

At one of the farewell dinners at the Lambert home, there was lots of reminiscing and rehashing of the highlights of the past year. One story led to another and somewhere, somehow, the Lucas case came up. The elder Lambert, as a member of the board of the United Black Fund, had been well aware of the Lucas pledge. It wasn't every day (or decade) that the Fund's leadership could revel in the promise of a ten thousand dollar gift—from an unexpected donor no less. They didn't revel for long.

"You might be interested in knowing," he told Simmie, "That that pledge was never paid. We sent him regular bills but they were apparently discarded and our phone messages were never answered. We finally just gave up on it."

Meredith Lambert had seen Simmie lose his cool. He had seen him hurt. He had seen him perturbed. Now, for the first time in their long and close association, he saw the clouds gather, the choler rise in his neck and face and then, Simmie simply exploded. He had been gulled. He had been violated. He had been raped.

"That son-of-a-bitch!" he screamed, "Sue him! I mean it! I want him sued! I demand it!"

He was adamant. He would not be put off. The elder Lambert argued that you just didn't do such things, but Simmie refused to listen and firmly stood his ground. And so, with many misgivings, the United Black Fund took Dr. William Lucas to court to sue him for the ten thousand dollars he had pledged over his attested and duly witnessed signature.

The rest is a matter of recorded local history and everyone in town knows the story. The case made the front pages and was the topic of the day. The court decided that the pledge was, in fact, a legal document and that the doctor was liable, making the decision the first and only time in the history of this city that a charitable institution had sued and collected an unpaid pledge.

Bill Lucas could well afford the ten thousand, but his failure in the operating room and his subsequent defeat in the courtroom cost him what no man can afford—his personal dignity, his reputation, his way of life.

And then there was his penury that compounded the price he was forced to pay. Lucas loved his money so passionately that his charity not only began in his home, it ended there. His largess was limited to the generous (by his measure) single dollar bills he self-righteously dropped on top of the dimes and quarters in his church's collection plate each Sunday. He had neither ear nor heart for causes—be they Alumni funds, museums, orchestras, the needy or the panoply of health drives. He was so unflappable in his refusal of any and every plea for help that in time his name had been scratched from almost all of the "hit" lists.

Suddenly all of that changed. Anyone who read the local papers learned that Dr. William Lucas, a leader in the city's ethnic community, had given a substantial gift to charity—incredible in itself—and the more so because the beneficiary was a fund for blacks. That became the signal for solicitors of every non-profit enterprise—legitimate and otherwise—to swoop down on him and buzz like hungry hornets anxious for the bite. His mailbox was gorged. His phone rang off the hook. He could find no peace.

His only option was to sacrifice the nourishing adulation of his bevy of patients for the anonymity of a bitter retirement; to sell off all of his office equipment and his luxury home, and crawl away to a distant city where his ignominy might not follow him.

To Dr. William Lucas, the public ostracism and his forced exodus were outrageously excessive punishment. But—to his fellow practitioners and to his fellow citizens—it was equitable retribution for his breach of the Hippocratic oath and for his breach of faith. The punishment did indeed fit the crime.

6

Live In Dignity

It wasn't easy finding sanctuary from the babel of the cocktail party, but—from the minute we spotted each other—Andy and I knew we had to rehash old times. It seemed like decades since our offices had been in the same building and we used to lunch together. Andy was an engineer, a graduate of Annapolis and "Old Navy" and he could spin some salty yarns about his service on the seas. Land operations were my part of the act. I'd had a rugged go during World War II as a Battalion Surgeon with an Armored Division in France and Germany. Now, ten years after the war had ended, we still enjoyed reliving and sharing the excitement of our combat days. And so—though we may not have qualified as social assets at the party, we sure were having a great reunion, reswapping the same old facts and fibs. Then it was cut short. I was called to the phone. It was my hospital resident, "Get here in a hurry, Doctor, Sidney Bennett has gone sour."

"I'll call you, Andy, we'll just have to get together." There were hurried apologies to my hostess, a quick word to my wife, and I was on my way.

As I was driving to the hospital, those few moments with Andy had surfaced so many of my war-time memories— long tucked away—that they began clicking off like slides on a screen. But the fun experiences seemed to be missing. Maybe it was because I was so preoccupied with what was ahead of me—that only the pictures of a single haunting sequence came back to me. I saw myself sitting in a grassy field at the foot of a bridge that spanned the Isar River, holding my head in my hands. The evening before, our battalion had moved up from Straubing to take a bridge and repair it for our tanks to cross the next morning. We had worked all night under gunfire from the other shore. By daylight the enemy had been silenced by a devastating cannonade and the bridge was ours and ready. The tanks had roared across, screaming south into Bavaria. The rest of the battalion and I tagged wearily behind after the sun had come up.

The field on the other side was a strew of fallen soldiers, each in his own grotesque posture of sudden bloody death. They were young faces—the skin on them was smooth. They were young bodies—the chests were full, the waists slim, the hands strong. But they were sullied and bloody young—not a breath in all. They were dead. All of the young were dead and all of the dead were young.

I saw and I mourned. I was too drained to weep. Nothing from Hippocrates could answer the questions I was asking myself. Why do we doctors pant in the chase for wisdom and cunning to save lives—all lives? Why do we have to struggle so to protect and support the defective, the infirm, the aged—to shield the last flicker of the flame of life against the gusts of time? And then, why did we permit the noble contest of war where the young were awarded death as their prize? And why, in these enlightened times of our mature society, were we culling—instead of the addled or the halt—only the elite specimens to feed into the maw of death? Why?

The bile of my memories was still bitter in my throat as I turned into the hospital parking lot, but there wasn't time now to dwell on nightmares or dawdle over imponderables. There was a job at hand. There was my oath to minister—at any time—to anyone. Tonight—it was Sidney Bennett.

Sidney Bennett's life had been one big good time. He had thrived in the double benison of health and success, and he loved fun—loved programming it and loved performing for it. He and his wife had traveled the world. They had toured the great çities, lolled at the fashionable resorts, and in any land or language, always attracted people and accumulated friends. Sidney Bennett thrilled to the majesty of the concert hall and to the fever of the racetrack, to the treasures of the museum and to the heroics of his grandson's Little League ballgame. Even in his seventies, he was preening himself each morning, going to his office for a couple of hours, lunching with "the boys" and then playing golf, watching a football game, or just chatting away the afternoon. Sidney Bennett bubbled in the froth of life, but he did penetrate the substance. He was devoted to his family and its responsibilities, and he accepted service to his community as a privilege. If he had enemies, they were silent. His friends were voluble.

Two years before, and completely without warning, he had suffered his first heart attack and I recall now how strange it had seemed to me at the time that it hadn't ruffled him. He actually accepted the commitment to bed and all the restraints with a kind of detachment. It wasn't until he was recuperating—when he had to face the limitations imposed by the damaging attack—that his complacency cracked. He had never known restriction and he just couldn't tolerate it. He puffed at half steam and he tottered in a feeble stab at resuming his former pace, coming to realize that he couldn't ever make it. The lights seemed to go out in those life-lusting eyes. His book had ended, the days of it were printless, numberless—just blank pages filling the binding.

And so he existed for a couple of years. Then, the night before I was called from the party, Sidney had his second coronary. He'd been awakened by oppressive pain in his chest. My first look at him dictated the diagnosis and the decisions. His sweaty ashen face and his shallow labored breathing told me the whole of his story. Over his protests, I called an ambulance to get him to the hospital immediately. There, his cardiogram spelled out the new attack. By the next afternoon, with the crutch of oxygen and pain-killing drugs, he was holding his own and, as I told the family, it was fifty-fifty. When the resident called me, I knew the odds had shifted to the wrong fifty.

When I reached the floor, I was puzzled by the deserted nurses' station. The answer was in the patient's room. I could hardly squeeze in. There were so many people scurrying and manipulating so much equipment that Sidney Bennett was barely visible. Nobody was talking, yet the room was full of sounds. There was the drone of the loudspeaker page, the crackling of the starched duck uniforms, the counterpoint of the wheezing machines. Bob, my resident, spotted me and edged me back out into the hall. His face was flushed. "We did it! We brought him back and now he's doing great."

"What happened?" I really didn't have to ask.

Triumphantly, Bob exploded: "At 8:20 the monitor quit bleeping. He'd had a cardiac arrest. The Chest Team was paged and we were all in the room within minutes. I got there first and jumped on his chest to give him artificial respiration until Pete, from Anesthesia, came to start the forced breathing machine. In the meantime we attached the pacemaker, and after the first few shocks, his heart was beating again."

I was listening to every word, but part of me was far away—in the grassy field on the banks of the Isar River—with the young who were dead. And the words went on— "It took about twenty minutes after the Levophed was going intravenously before we could get a decent sustained blood pressure reading, and that's when we had our first opportunity to notify you. His heart had stopped! He was dead! And we brought him back!"

He could hardly contain himself, but with a hand on his shoulder, I halted his gush of words. "Bob, what did you really do for this man?" He just stood there, mouth open, stunned. I pushed my way past him back to the bedside and looked down at what the Team had retrieved.

I surveyed my fine old friend, lying naked, exposed to anyone willing to look. His body and his bed linen were a mess of drying blood. There hadn't been time to be neat. The oxygen tube was secured to his nose and was hissing in his nostrils. His fine shock of white hair was like a kitchen mop. His pillow was wet with the sweat that had rolled down his face, sopping the bindings of the breathing machine that were left under his neck. The soiled cotton wrapping blanket—raised from the bottom and lowered from the top to accommodate all the life-holding fixings—was wadded up around his waist, the only uninvaded part of his body. Wires ran in snaking confusion from his arms and legs connecting them to the pacemaker and electrocardiograph machines. His right arm was taped to a board to steady the intravenous needle that was giving the nutritive fluid, drip by drip, from a bottle suspended over the bed. A retention catheter was draining off the waste fluid from his bladder, emptying it into a plastic sac hanging near the floor. Instinctively, I reached for his wrist. His pulse was full and regular. His eyes were closed peacefully, his breathing was rhythmic and easy. His skin was warm and dry, and his color was normal. Sidney Bennett's vital signs were all good. He'd been the beneficiary of a medical miracle, saved by a network of tubes, wires and machines, by blood, glucose and oxygen. He breathed and he lived because of the combined talent and sweat of five medical specialties; because every doctor and every nurse in that room had pooled training and skill to reverse the irreversible—and not one of them even knew Sidney Bennett. He was an anonymous human, a patient in need, and they had responded without questioning. Now they stood there, almost in a paralysis of exhaustion and exhilaration, beholding their awesome achievement.

I didn't know this man either. The Sidney Bennett I had known was the goer, the doer, the Sidney Bennett of the dapper suit and the fresh boutonniere. Now, it broke my heart to look down on this wisp of a man, this remnant, sustained by needle and drained by tube, supported by electric shock and mucked in his own secretions.

I wanted desperately to cover his nakedness, hide all his ugliness. I wanted to penetrate his limbo. I wanted to be able to just reassure my friend. Out of habit the words fell, "Hello, Sidney, how do you feel?" They were hollow, vacuous, only rhetorical words, but they did make contact. Little by little, his lids drew up and his eyes—awake and aware and angry—fixed their stare on me. Even before he spoke, I thought I knew what they were saying. Then he opened his mouth, slowly tongued his lips, and in a hoarse but clear condemnation demanded, "How could you do this to me?" In a strange amalgam of senselessness and feelings, of subconscious and conscious—he couldn't stand being witness to his own death and unwanted resurrection, and powerless to resist either. He held me fixed in his flagellating glare, making me unable to escape his strangling punishment.

"How could you do this to me?", he asked again, and when I started to parry his question, his lids slid down and peremptorily shut me out. He too must have known that I had no answer. I laid his hand back on the bed and walked out of the room. In the hallway, Bob was giving rapid fire instructions to his intern on the precautions and medications to be taken in the next few hours. My appearance braked him in. He stopped short in the middle of a sentence and just stood there looking at me—half puzzled, half nettled at the anger and anguish in my face. How could I be so displeased? My patient had been dead and now he was alive, and *he* and *his* team had done it!

I hadn't really meant to be so unfeeling. "You did a fine job, Bob. It's thrilling—this marvel you performed—and you all deserve congratulations. But I have to ask you again, to what purpose? Bob, what did you accomplish? I know you didn't have a spare second to analyze or appraise what you were doing. You reacted by reflex and you acted by rote. You worked over Sidney Bennett for close to an hour, but did you really see him? He's cut and stained and shamefully exposed. His cardiograms showed you that he doesn't have enough heart muscle left to sustain him in any kind of lifestyle. He won't even be able to breathe without help. He has worn out all that is vital and now he is entitled to go to his peace—in dignity, Bob—in dignity—as a human being, not like a lab animal wrenched back to its rack of exhaustion and struggle in the cause of medical progress. No, I'm not preaching euthanasia. You know we don't subscribe to that. If he had a shred of a chance, we'd be honor-bound to give him all we have and all we know, but this man is sapped, he's at the end of his line, and all you've done is lend him another inch of suffering."

Bob swallowed hard. I think he began to understand.

"Should we quit now?"

"No, we don't quit. You've come too far for us to stop now. Keep the I.V. and the oxygen going and make sure he is comfortable. At this point, you have no choice but to give him even the remotest chance to make the grade. If he can do it on his own, let's help him, but if he can't, don't 'shock' him again."

I was in a drugged kind of sleep when the phone rang around 4 A.M. It was Bob.

"Doctor—Sidney Bennett just passed away—in dignity."

7

A Night In The Attic

Nobody ever seemed to care why they called her "Billy". Why she had buried "Bernice" on the way to school the first day of first grade was her secret, her own declaration of independence—precociously and prematurely. But—nobody seemed to care.

My phone rang around 4 A.M. It was Billy's father, first apologizing for waking me, and then telling me how very concerned he was about Billy's sudden illness.

Generally, I could accept night calls with grace. I get a lot of them. Having to get dressed and go out in the middle of the night—much less a zero night—had me grousing. This time, though, I really had no choice. Billy's parents were longtime patients and longtime friends—first-name good friends, and I knew that they would never disturb me if there were no urgency.

Billy had a terrible bellyache, he told me, with nausea, a fever, and acute pain in the right lower abdomen. Her mom had tried all the simple remedies, but nothing worked. Billy was crying hysterically and her parents were frantic. Yes, of course, I would come right over.

I groaned my way out of bed and into my clothes; pants, shirt, jacket and necktie. Always a necktie, no matter the time of day or night. A fearful patient looking up at his physician for help has to see a figure of substance and bearing for reassurance. Yes, always a necktie.

It didn't take long. Billy's folks lived closeby. They were waiting for me in the doorway of their expansive expensive new home—undressed in their nightclothes, wearing the worried look of the anxious parents that they had cause to be.

"Billy is up in the attic".

The attic, I knew, had been added to their original building plans as a playroom or "get-away" room for the kids. When her brother left for college, Billy couldn't wait to lug up her sleeping bag and take over the attic as her own private domain—her very own atelier.

In her early teen years, Billy had discovered her flair for color and form and became more and more absorbed in the arts. After a short romance with sketching and paint, she found her true love in fabrics and pattern. She began weaving wool structures, first with classical materials and then, with exotic and bizarre bits and shreds of colored rags that she could blend into artistic designs.

I knew Billy as a bright intense young lady who seemed to enjoy school and the normal learning process, but not her schoolmates in the usual peer relationships that often consume kids at this age. Instead, she relished the freedom of her solitude and the joys of her colorful warping and woofing. She apparently had some talent and had won prizes in exhibitions at school.

It was at this time in her life, age 15/16, that the call for help had come. With her mother and father leading the way, I trudged up the two flights of stairs and then stopped short at the top. The weirdly discordant scene was out of a horror movie. Billy's agonizing groans were bouncing off the multicolored fabrics streaming down from the rafters. I felt as if I were in a cavern of stalactites pointing their ragged fingers at that anguished body, curled up and contorting on the floor.

Billy quieted down and gave a straightforward history of nausea coming on soon after dinner, then the feeling of fever, then pain all over her abdomen that eventually moved down to settle as an aching focus in the right lower quadrant. She held her belly with both hands and moaned in pain and fear. I asked a lot of other questions, but the story remained simple, a rather classic description of an acute appendicitis.

I had to get down on my knees to examine her in her position on the floor. Very carefully, I ran my hands over her abdomen, all the time watching her eyes for reaction to various pressures. Yes, it hurt when I bore down over the appendix, and yes, she did flinch when I went a little deeper in my probing, but somehow, the signs didn't ring true. There was no spasm, no rebound, and at this point, Billy looked more puzzled than sick. I took her temperature and it was normal. No longer moaning, Billy was watching my every move with an intense questioning stare. I climbed back to my feet, and turning to the anxious parents who had been standing by watching the whole diagnostic exercise, I gave my verdict.

"My friends, there is nothing wrong with your Billy."

"Not appendicitis?"

"No. There are no signs of appendicitis."

"Then what is the problem?"

"Perhaps you'd better ask Billy."

Billy sat up, and with a brazenly smirking grin, gave up her charade of illness.

"I know you've been treating my father for his high blood pressure and I've really been worried about him. I also know that you doctors think more about your expensive cars, your country clubs and your golf scores than you do about your patients. So—I thought I'd put you to the test. I just wanted to make sure that you weren't that kind of a doctor and that you cared enough about my father to come to him if he needed you—even in the middle of the night."

"Billy", I said, "it was a great scheme and you acted it out very well. And yes, I'll take care of your father—whenever—but, as for you, you had better find yourself another doctor."

I couldn't hide my anger. I stomped out and drove home, dreading the long sleepy day of work that lay ahead.

8

A Broken Promise

It is only of passing interest to most, but for those of us in the medical profession, the Obit columns in the daily papers are must reading, an accounting of the patients who have left us—in one way or another. And so it was not surprising that the one-line listing of Sarah (Mrs. Henry) Huxley's death caught my eye. It had only been a few months since her son had died—suddenly and unexpectedly. At that time word had filtered through to me via family friends that Mrs. Huxley had been so distressed over her son Edward's death that she had withdrawn completely from everyone, everything, and now, obviously from life itself. Was her mourning really that devastating, that honest? With all that I had learned about the Huxley family, I had my doubts.

Edward's death was given more extensive coverage than his mother's one-liner. I couldn't forget the shocking headline: "Prominent Physician—A Suicide" and in reduced print: "Edward W. Huxley, Promising Young Internist, Found Dead In Bed". What an eye-popper before the morning coffee! It was a straight news story with no inferences. The Doctor's housekeeper, usually off over the weekend, had arrived at 8 on Monday morning. Lights were on all over the house and the sound of television was coming from the bedroom. The Doctor, who was usually finishing his breakfast by now, was nowhere to be seen. She called out to him, then knocked on his bedroom door. No response.

Thinking he might have been called out during the night for an emergency, she gingerly unlatched his door. There he was—stretched out in his bed, his eyes wide open in a ghastly stare focussed on a spot on the ceiling. She had never seen a dead man, yet she knew this man was dead. In a panic she raced out of his room and bee-lined to the phone in the library to call the police.

The Police blotter stated that an almost empty Seconal bottle, tipped over on the bedside table along with half a quart of gingerale, was found beside the very dead Dr. Huxley. The Coroner's report read: "Death probably occurred between Friday evening and Saturday morning. The Doctor had apparently stuffed handfuls of the 'red devils' into his mouth and flushed them down with swigs of gingerale. The body was found haunched on the bed fully clothed. Only the shoes had been kicked off. Otherwise the room was neat and orderly with everything in its usual place. No note was found."

Strangely enough, there was no follow-up in the papers the next day or ever after. It seemed obvious that someone high-up had slammed the lid closed on a bubbling kettle. There wasn't even a formal death notice.

I had only seen E. W. Huxley, M.D. a few times, but I remembered him as a fine looking man, thin and slightly built with a twinge of the reddish freckled complexion he must have inherited from his Irish mother. He was very serious looking except for a wry little smile. He spoke softly but in a hurried tempo. He was always impeccably tailored in expensive yet elegantly understated clothes. His carriage was noble. He was a most impressive-appearing gentleman.

By reputation, I knew him as an internist with excellent credentials; a graduate of the Johns Hopkins Medical School who had been trained at the most prestigious clinics and medical centers of the country. After his internship at Hopkins, he moved from one residency to another; in internal medicine, cardiology and gastroenterology. Instead of training for a career, it appeared that "training" was to be his career. That's why so many of us were surprised to hear that he was finally about to break out of the womb of institutional learning and was coming home to bite the bullet of private practice in internal medicine.

First came the rumor and then the reality of "the second coming": Edward's p. r.—either familial or professional (we never did find out which) was brilliant. Everything short of trumpets blared "the return of the native". The medical giant, who had honed his skills at the feet of the greatest gurus of medicine, was now going to heal the bent and the broken, preach the gospel of good health, share his accrued wisdom with the hometown folks.

But why would someone with his "status" medical background compromise with an appointment at a middle-rung hospital that offered no accredited teaching service? And— when he did open his doors for business—why did he seem to go out of his way to avoid one and all of us at our Medical Center and at the University Hospital? We had so many unanswered questions.

Huxley settled himself in a rather large and imposing downtown office and in a fashionable suburban home. According to the ladies' bridge circuit, he hired the city's most expensive decorator to select and coordinate every detail and the result, according to their unquestioned authority, was the penultimate.

His personal affairs really weren't for us to judge, but being brothers of the World War II fraternity of M.D.s who had to work their way up, we couldn't help resenting this show of opulence. Could someone be underwriting Edward or was there a bank willing to gamble on his success and lend him this much money? Our guesswork was, of course, tinged with more than a touch of jealousy.

What was also bruited about was that Huxley's phone rang off the hook from the day he hung out his shingle, and before long, people were complaining about how difficult it was to get an appointment. Although none of us had reason to pronounce him God's gift to the local medical scene, his clientele, apparently, were satisfied customers. Dr. Huxley was handsome, single, and the new boy on the block—none of which detracted from his appeal—especially to the women. And how could a patient not be impressed with the museum-like gallery of diplomas—embossed with the golden names of Lahey, Mayo and Cleveland Clinic—covering the walls of his office? Actually, a closer look at them bared the tertiary levels of his affiliations with those exalted fountainheads. They were more in the nature of attending fellowships than positions of responsibility. Whatever—people flocked to his office and in time, there wasn't one of us who hadn't lost patients to him.

With this luminous reputation confirmed by a successful practice, Huxley should have been a most happy man. On the ledger of achievement, he had it all. Then why—in less than one year after opening his office—did he take his life?

For days after his death, the doctors at our hospital and the rest of the town were abuzz with rumors and speculations. After all—Edward had grown up in our neighborhoods, gone to school with many of us. Others of us had had social or business relations with members of his family. The more I heard about him and those around him, the more intrigued I became with the unfolding familial pattern. Gossip was never my indulgence. Still I found myself almost magnetized to the pursuit and the unravelling of all the details I could unearth. When the facts pieced together, they could have been spooned out of the plot of a Dickens novel.

The Huxleys were Anglo-Irish immigrants. When he was six, Henry, Edward's father came to America with his father, who made his exit in a great and mysterious hurry. He left a dying wife in her bed and a process-server standing on the wharf, shaking a fistful of papers as the ship sailed out of port. Edward's mother, Sarah, also "came over" as a youngster, but from a poverty-level potato farm somewhere in Ireland. Even in the land of plenty, neither of them were able to get beyond the 8th grade. Papa went to work for a junk dealer, tending his horse, loading and unloading his wagon. When she was only a young teenager, Mama's initiation into the work force was stitching blouses in a sweatshop.

Sarah and Henry met at a street-corner bazaar on the steamy lower Eastside of New York. Each found the other a welcome listener to shared frustrations and dreams. Their relationship didn't flower into any emotion akin to love, but with no available alternatives, the couple drifted closer and closer together. After some months of dating and the inevitable and increasing intimacies, they agreed that marriage was their brightest option. The wedding was very simple; the honeymoon very short; a hotel room on Saturday night and Sunday; back to work on Monday morning.

Some months later, Henry's boss decided—with his business flourishing so successfully—he was ready for the big time in scrap. That necessitated a move to the midwest to get closer to the hub of the steel industry and there open a yard. He offered Henry the opportunity of going with him. There was so little joy for the newlyweds in New York and, with their family strings mostly untied, they jumped at the chance for clean air and a new life.

Once settled in this burgeoning middle west city, they melted into a neighborhood group that shared playgrounds and schools and social gettogethers—all the bits and pieces that form a small community.

Huxley's fortunes rose and fell with the price of scrap and the demand for it. At first he worked exclusively for the man who had brought him, but as soon as he could afford his own wagon, he went into business for himself—after a fashion—still keeping his boss as his prime outlet. While the boss moved on to the greener fields of a large yard to store his scrap and hold it for sale to the mills by the ton, Henry—with neither the goals nor the entrepreneurial skills—was content to continue combing the streets and back alleys for his odds and ends of iron and steel.

Meanwhile, Sarah ran the home show. She was a wiry little woman with a sharp pointed nose that jutted out between her freckled tight drawn cheeks. She had the mien and the coloring of an Irish woman, but with piercing eyes that were hers alone—eyes that had the intensity of a hound on the chase. She was never satisfied with the monies her man brought home, but she never complained. She kept her house shipshape, the children scrubbed to a shine. She managed her brood like an army sergeant. She knew not to ask for help from Henry, and she got little of it. He was free to roam the roads plying his trade until dark. It was like a game to him. He had a native talent for what he was doing and he loved every minute of it, but not as much as the Saturday nights out that Sarah generously permitted him. That's when he had license to drink with his buddies at the corner saloon until either his money or his tolerance ran out. Sunday was his day to share in the household chores. But— there must have been other "sharing times". He did sire six children.

For the insight into what ultimately became the drive and direction of the Huxley family, one would have to eavesdrop on the story Sarah once confided to a close friend. Back in Ireland, when she was only eight or nine, she accompanied her mother on an errand to the Manor House, the home of their landlord and master. While her Mom was exchanging gossip with the maids in the kitchen, Sarah sneaked off through the butler's door into the great hall. She couldn't believe what she was seeing. The ceilings were as high as the heavens with their hundreds of lights sparkling like stars from the candles of the ornate chandeliers. Huge gilt-framed portraits of the Manor's ancestors were on every wall, and as she moved from one to the next, she was mesmerized by the nobility of their postures and the elegance of their regal dress. And the chairs below were like miniature thrones covered with gorgeous fabrics. She couldn't help running her fingers over the lush silken brocades. She tingled to their touch. As she came to an opening to the garden, she heard voices and peeped through the trellised gates. There, hostessing over the most beautiful tea service, was the Lady of the Manor entertaining her friends. Their dress, their mannerisms—it was all part of a tableau that would be permanently etched in her memory—a vision of the life she dreamed would one day be hers. Aping their stance and their gestures, her mother's voice snatched her back to her real world.

With her face wrapped in a rough woolen shawl to damp the sting of the biting wind, Sarah slogged the muddy road to the cold and dreary hut that she had to call home. She tightened her jaw, she clenched her fists and she solemnly swore to herself that somehow, somewhere—she knew not when—she would be noble and rich and matriarch of a like dynasty of patricians.

And that was the obsession that propelled Sarah into the modus vivendi of the family she had bred. Her first child was a girl—unappreciated, almost unwanted. (Girls do not promulgate a dynasty.) The child was tolerated with some measure of kindness, taught only domestic tasks, and at 16, was shuttled off to a counter job in a neighborhood bakery shop. With no recourse, there she stayed, adding the bulk of her pay to help prop up the family budget.

The second was also a girl and a second disappointment. Never encouraged—neither at school nor at home—her only graduation was from a 9th grade classroom to the cutting loft of a mens' clothing factory.

Number three child (Sarah was popping them out every year and a half) was a boy, and that brought hope and direction to the mother's master plan. For the first time, school, education, study became the buzzwords in the Huxley family's vocabulary. But—it didn't play out. No matter how severely Sarah pressured and prodded both him and his teachers, the boy barely squeezed through each grade to finish high school. Then—thanks to the push and pull of one of Papa's drinking buddies—he was slipped through the back door into the State University. When he realized that he had to help support himself, he chose an after-school job behind the bar of a corner saloon. His classwork was far above him. The bar was more on his level and much more fun so that it wasn't long before the great white Huxley hope gave up his books for the barroom, and Mother, in despair, gave up on that chapter of her life work.

Number four was a girl, but one to whom Sarah reacted differently. This little girl was a beauty. She had inherited the most handsome features of each of her parents and matured into a bright and appealing young lady. Never an A student, she was the first of the children to graduate high school on her own ability and momentum. Working her job at a lumber yard, she met a promising young salesman, fell in love, and before Sarah could convincingly protest the liaison, she ran off and married.

Never aware of how apt it would be, the Huxleys had named this third daughter "Goldie". Shortly after their marriage, Goldie's go-go husband sensed the promise of the impending construction boom. Risking his neck and their future, he borrowed heavily from the banks and bought up large tracts of undeveloped land. He used the land as collateral and proceeded to bring in water lines and electricity, divided his acreage into streets and lots and built groups of homes in clusters. They sold like hot cakes at the fair. Young families and their children moved in and they needed schools. The shopping malls were next. He was a slick operator and lucky too to get in on the first swell of the greatest real estate boom of the decade and then ride the crest of the wave all the way beyond his wildest dreams.

This was fulfillment (at least partial) of Sarah Huxley's dreams too. It was a first score—one of her brood had made it. She basked in the rays of Goldie's affluence and bragged to anyone who would listen about her daughter's palatial home, designer clothes, society balls and the less apparent trappings of the rich and famous.

Goldie's largesse was as unstinting for her family as it was for the charities that she calculated would bring her a hefty return in social benefits. But—generously as she gave dollars to ease the life of her poor relatives, she never gave of herself. She excluded them from her fancy parties, hid them from her "celebrity" friends. They were beneficiaries of her money but not of her time or her heart.

Backtracking to Sarah's childbearing activity, her fifth child was another boy—a clone of Papa—a big strong body sheltering a limited mind. He quit school at 16 to become a carpenter's apprentice, graduating to the dubious distinction of membership in the Union and later lucking out with a small but secure corner in Goldie's husband's empire.

Even after five "misses" and the enervating burden of raising a brood of young children, Sarah's sights never strayed from her target. With prayers for a turn in her birthing fortunes she once again became pregnant. When the third Huxley son was born, one look and Sarah knew instantly she'd hit gold. There was no question about naming him. Over Henry's protest, the boy was christened Edward Wales Huxley after England's crown prince—the name certain to befit its bearer, certain to insure his nobility. Edward—with his mother's coloring and features—was the first child to totally resemble her, and this too seemed predictive of a life of aspiration and accomplishment.

From the day he was born, Edward was the sole focus of Sarah's attentions and affections. While he flowered in the sunshine of her loving indulgences, the older children were almost neglected—to grow like weeds in the garden. Strangely, rather than resent this obvious partiality they accepted their baby brother as the prince their mother had enthroned him, giving him love and devotion equal to hers. This did make for a peaceful contented household, but not of the traditional variety.

That all changed one Saturday night. Sarah was nursing little Edward, humming in contentment—almost like a first-time mother—when Henry burst through the door, obviously and totally tanked up. His pants were wide open with his exposed organ standing at full mast. He tore the baby from her breast, tossed him into his crib and lunged at Sarah lasciviously. Like a tiger in a fury, she jumped up, grabbed a broom and savagely slammed the handle across Henry's face. The pain of his shattered nose and the spate of blood sobered him into instant retreat. Sarah ran after him, still wildly swinging the broom and screaming, "If you ever try to touch me again, I'll chop your thing off with a meat cleaver. And if you ever touch that child again, I'll kill you dead."

That was the end of Henry's home bed privileges. But he lost no time in finding sexual solace in other beds. There were always the hungry widows and willing wives of absentee or abstaining husbands. So long as most of his paycheck kept the family afloat, neither Sarah nor the older children seemed to care much about his philandering—not even when they would overhear the neighborhood gossips gorging on the sorties of Henry, the "Alley Cat".

More and more, Henry was seen less and less until he became a virtual stranger in his own home. And when some years later—an angry cuckold put a knife in his chest—that was the end of his sexual escapades—and his life. The truth be told, he was neither mourned nor missed.

With a plethora of kids and a paucity of dollars, Sarah was a very busy lady. Even with household work assignments for each child, there was always a surplus of cleaning and laundering left for her. She did all the sewing, mending and patching—all the retreading of one child's discards to fit the next one. As for the marketing, she wouldn't trust that job to anyone. Her haggling was the scourge of the shopkeepers. She would smell a fresh bread and insist it was yesterday's and should be discounted. She would argue that a piece of prime priced meat was really a second cut. She would finger the salad greens until they crinkled enough to be worth less than labelled. To Sarah's credit, though, she always paid cash on the line, and her scouting and skimping did ease her through good times and bad.

Stew—for economy's sake—was the mainstay of the family diet. With the large pot crooked in one arm she would circle the table ladling out a portion for each child, meticulously fishing out more of the meat chunks for Edward and more of the vegetable flotsam for the others.

Edward Wales Huxley was the "chosen" in all family departments. He was always dressed in new clothes—never the hand-me-downs. He was the only one to have his own room "so he could have a quiet place to study", Mama explained. Whether it was that privacy or his genes—Edward loved to read, loved to learn and was the first and only of the children to do well in school, apparently without effort.

With the older members of the family marrying and producing assorted children of their own, Sarah's band expanded. As it did, however, her interest in them seemed to contract. In astonishingly un-grandmotherish fashion, she was almost indifferent to her childrens' children. She was exclusively devoted to her last-born, watching him, guiding him and guarding him in every step of his development.

Edward, after navigating the hazardous pre-med curriculum of one of the better state colleges, graduated with an acceptable—not exceptional record. Four years later he received his M.D. from Johns Hopkins and opted to do his internship there. From then on—it was the strange sequence of churning in the training pools of one prestigious medical facility after another until the day he took the long overdue plunge into the actual practice of medicine.

Sarah never publicly took bows for the instant success of her eminent son, the doctor, though she must have beemed to herself over her success. But now she had another dream, another goal. Edward was getting older and time was running out for the start of a family. She was convinced that only from his seed could a Huxley noble lineage be cultivated and the family's continuity be perpetuated. At first her approach to him was timorous and stumbling, and Edward's response was evasive and fumbling. When she finally told him that he needed to seriously market himself to the eligible and desirable young ladies of the city, he was cornered with no choice but to acquiesce, promising what he knew he could never honor. How could he tell his mother that he was never attracted to women? How could he tell her that all of his erotic dreams had always been related to men and that only his basic timidity and the fear of social censure and rebuff had kept him from the homosexual chase? How could he so denude himself and so devastate the mother whose entire world revolved around him?

Was it this social conflict that ultimately demolished him? Or was it the repetitive current of anxiety and fear that ran so transparently through his medical notes? How strange that it was his death that illuminated the dark passages of his life. The first forbidding omen was in a beautifully tooled bronze wall plaque, a piece of his office furnishings that were put up for sale after his death. It read: "Physician beware, A human life hangs on thine every word." The second clue was concealed in the medical records of Dr. Edward Wales Huxley. Those were transferred to my office for the patients—some of whom had previously left me for his care and others whom I had never seen before—who now had made appointments with me. He had dictated his meticulous notes into a machine and then they were typed into the patients' records, carefully divided under the captions "Complaints", "Past History", "Physical Findings", "Lab Reports", and "Xray Findings". What disturbed me the most were the contents of the final category, "Impressions and Plans".

He would translate each symptom that each patient described into the spector of a fatal disease. A cough, he noted, could be tuberculosis of the lungs; a belly cramp could indicate the start of a cancer of the stomach; a headache could be caused by a growing brain tumor. Apparently, Huxley was so obsessed that—even the negative reports of the endless diagnostic tests he ordered—didn't calm his fears. His end page notes read, "Mr. A's chest films look clear but he still could have an infection that didn't show on the xray. Plan—must watch very carefully and repeat film in a month". Or, "Mrs. B's diarrhea is responding to medication, but this could very well develope into an ulcerative colitis." Always, always there was the pervading dread that his patient might be harboring a dangerous illness. He seemed to be consumed by the fear of catastrophe befalling each and every one who had entrusted his care to him. Edward's patients, quite understandably, were most impressed with his thoroughness, never even suspecting what drove him to such overzealous attentions. They never read his pain.

No wonder this man hid out for so many years in institutional fortresses. When finally he thought he had conquered his phobia of causing a patient's disability or death—through error of omission or commission—he accepted the cloak of practicing physician. Wthin months, though, the weight of that responsibility evidently became more than he could sustain, and he took his escape through the only vent he saw open to him.

The last news of the Huxley family came to me via a close friend of theirs and mine. He was one of the very few privy to the proceedings at Edward's graveside. "We were a small group huddling together in a freezing rain waiting for Mama to arrive so the service could begin", he told me. "Way after the appointed time, the long black undertaker's limousine pulled up and—ahead of Edward's brothers and sisters—Sarah got out. She was sheathed and veiled in black, but you could still see her face, so wan and wizened, her body so shrunken and frail. We were all transfixed by the icy look on this dry-eyed tragic figure. She walked slowly but directly to the rim of the grave. She stared down into the hole for what seemed like hours. Then she slowly raised her veil, leaned forward, worked her mouth and spit its load, splatting on the casket that now cradled her adored prodigy. She pulled her veil down over her face, pivoted to turn her back on the grave and walked alone back to the car—without waiting for the burial rites. None of us will ever forget that scene."

The friend who told me this story, didn't really know the Huxley family long or well enough to understand this performance. He had no way of knowing that for Sarah it wasn't only her son who was to be buried. It was herself, her drives, her dreams, her whole life were being entombed in that hole—forever and ever.

Nor could anyone ever understand the life-sized oil portrait that was found stored away in the Huxley attic. It was Sarah, gowned in regal red velvet with a jabot of white lace at her throat. Inscribed on the brass nameplate in elegant script was "Sarah Cluny Huxley". A woman bought it at a housesale. She wanted to use the frame for a mirror.

9

Fall From Olympus

"Thanks, coach . . ."

The nurse attending the patient in the next bed turned and stopped to listen. The gaunt hawk-like face on the pillow didn't move. The lids were clamped tight—but in the voice and the words—there was the excitement of a wide-eyed youngster.

"Right! We sure nailed 'em bad. . . . Aw, coach, it wasn't only me. . . . I'm just lucky to have the greatest legs. All our guys were great. . . . the best in England, but thanks anyway. . . . Brighton? Don't worry, coach, we'll be ready for those Brighton chaps all right. . . . all right."

The room was quiet again and the nurse walked back to her hall station. As she fingered the rack for the right chart, she reported to the night supervisor, "Romansky in 17 is out in left field again." Into the nurses' notes she wrote, "Patient disoriented, but apparently in no distress. No change in vital signs."

I don't know what it was that made Sanford Romansky one of my favorite patients. Intellectually, spiritually, economically, he was pure middle class. Through the years of our doctor-patient relationship, I had seen him plod without inspiration through his term as a construction plumber, and then graduate without flurry into the social security register.

Sanford had a wife, Ruth. I'd met her several times and yet she was without definition in my memory. She was colorless, shapeless, with only the ordinary virtue of not being extraordinary.

In the early days of their marriage she may have been the fair damsel to her knight-in-armor, but no gesture or word between them ever clued me. By the time I knew the couple, theirs was a relationship of habit. I heard that when their children were grown, Mrs. Romansky, quite by accident, took a job as a billing clerk with a furnace repair company. It became her refuge from housework, and the small additional income was such a help that she continued working even after Sanford retired.

Perhaps it was the very lackluster of his life that sent Sanford into orbits of reminiscence or fantasy on the flimsiest provocation. I never could make the distinction. Once I asked him how he happened to become a plumber in America. He ducked the question; the details apparently had been scrapped as unneeded or a to-be-hidden agenda. When he reported the marriages of his children or any event that is usually considered memorable in family life, it was always in the chilled factual prose of a news clipping. But when he blow-by-blowed the triumphs of his heroic young athlete's life in the little London outpost of Hove, his recounting was breathless and blazing. Was it the passing years that made his tales grow taller? Or was it his famished ego that draped his feats in fable? It really didn't matter. The little man who now was always sitting-in my office, at home in front of television—just sitting everywhere—had once been a great runner. Handsome and lithe-limbed and fleet, he'd been the local hero of every track meet and then the fastest delivery boy in town. It was he who had put the Hove soccer team on the map! To authenticate his past triumphs, Sanford would happily share his hallowed yellowed clippings with anyone who showed even the slightest interest.

That was long ago—long before Sanford developed diabetes with the associated clogged arteries in his legs. Under periodic supervision, he and his diabetes had been equally easy to control. That was until a foreboding black spot on his big toe brought him to my office. Within a week the sore broke down and the large open ulcer that resulted necessitated his hospitalization.

Sanford took to the heat cradle and the complete bed rest as though they were part of the indulgent regime of a spa hotel. He became the gay blade of Ward B, holding happy court for anyone who had the time to dawdle at his bedside to share a laugh or listen to some peppered story. Even the staff doctors and nurses warmed to Sanford, and Sanford basked. His ulcer, unfortunately, was not as responsive. Not only did it not heal; it grew and it festered. A large contiguous vein became involved and thrombosed, then broke down to form a disturbing sinus.

As his pain heightened, his spirits sagged. Interns, nurses, orderlies, maids—all of us tried to cheer him. It was a mockery. The kinder we were to him, the uglier he was to us. Visiting him each day was more than a professional frustration. It was the odium of being battered by his condemnations; of the hospital diet, the heavy-handed nurses, the slow response of the attendants—of every complaint in the syndrome of the unhappy patient. I grew to despise Sanford Romansky as much as those damned ulcers on his foot.

As time went on, there were a few brief interludes of cooperation and pleasantness, but those only punctuated the endless hours of see-sawing between vituperation and resignation. Sanford gradually gave up the fight. He spoke only when spoken to, and then only in the curt "yes" and "no" of the witness stand.

Finally, after weeks of careful ministrations and painfully slow progress, the inflammation did subside. Although it could have taken months before they would granulate back to healing, the ulcerated areas at least dried up. Sanford still wasn't well enough to leave the hospital, but I had to chance it in the hope that a home environment might polish away the tarnish of depression that had tainted him as devastatingly as had his disease. There also was the optimistic possibility that a change of scene could accelerate the recovery of the whole man.

The morning of Sanford's scheduled discharge I hurried to 17. After all his carping about the hospital, I was sure that he would be singing hallelujah, but not even a smile slit the glaze of that sullen face. "No," he said, "I'm not leaving here."

I asked "why" a dozen times in a dozen different ways.

There was only a simple answer, "I'll stay until I'm out of bed and walking." Sanford closed his eyes and that dropped the curtain on the conversation.

During the long course of their father's illness, I'd had several conferences with Sanford's son and daughter. Mrs. Romansky, somehow, never seemed to be available. Now Sanford's behavior had me so completely baffled that I turned to his children again. They came to my office, fidgeted through my explanations, evading any response except for sneaking glances at each other. Finally the daughter broke into an uneasy silence that had become even too stifling for them. She stammered, "You see, Doctor, my parents don't get along . . . at all . . . they fight . . . they fight fiercely with each other . . . she says terrible things to him . . . Anyway there'd be nobody at home to care for him . . . she works all day . . . Do you understand? They just can't get along . . . it would be impossible . . . she would kill him with her words. We can't spell them out. You'll just have to believe us. She would kill him with her words."

Quote by quote, the children confided the heated, hated epithets that had become the father-mother tongue of the house. The pattern was all too familiar—the inability of one mate to accept illness and dependency in the other. What evidently had never been a great love had degenerated into a deep and fixed revulsion. The job that once had been a happy escape for Ruth now was the onerous necessity of supporting an inadequate. She pitied herself. She detested him. Why should she be chained to this disease-ridden hulk who was clinging to his invalidism just to plague her to death? She stung, she bit, and the venom diffused through his sensitive flesh. As much as Sanford detested his union with his hospital bed, the prospect of a reunion with his licensed mate was even more terrifying. Being able to walk—to walk out of the house—to get away when he could no longer abide the lashing was an imperative for him.

Another week, another conference. In every spare moment between patient cases and crises, I tried to penetrate the alleys of alternatives that the Romansky family had blinded. Compounding these problems were the hospital expenses. Moving Sanford to City Hospital was the first option I pursued because I thought that the change of scenery and personnel and the relief from financial pressures might be a solution.

Yes, if the admitting officer, after seeing him, would approve, they would accept him for admission as a charity patient. Sanford agreed readily and was transferred by ambulance to what seemed to be the only gate of hope left open to him.

I couldn't get Sanford out of my thoughts. Had they accepted him at City? No one had contacted me. That afternoon, after going back to the hospital to check an acutely ill patient, I dashed up to his room and then froze at the door. There he was—just a blob of gray in a wadding of white—his face gelled in the desperate resolute stare of a captain looking out to sea from the bridge of his sinking ship.

"What happened?" I blurted out.

"I'll tell you what happened. Two Docs examined me—one was the head of surgery and the other a regular medical doctor like you. And then the two of 'em started to argue what to do with me. The surgeon was the big honcho, I guess, and he said I could only stay there if I let 'em cut off my leg. 'If that leg of yours ever heals,' " he said, " 'I guarantee it won't stay healed. Maybe it'll take months, but it's got to bust down again.' " So—Sanford gulped, took a deep breath and went on, " 'So'—he said 'we gotta take that rotting thing off and get you out of bed and up and moving.' He musta seen I wasn't buying that idea, and he kinda deiced. 'We can probably save the knee,' he said, ' Give you a better prosthesis and you'll be jumping aroun' like a cricket in no time.' "

There was a long pause. "He can't have my leg." The fierce light in Sanford's eyes had faded into a pathetic stare. It was a wordless plea for rescue. I couldn't help thinking how that "big honcho surgeon" didn't know about the track meets in Hove and the soccer victories and the pictures in the local paper. If he had, how could he deplume Sanford Romansky of what he coveted most? I could say nothing. I had no answers. I just knew that I had to get to a phone to call City to corroborate what Sanford had told me. It was promptly confirmed. The chief offered no compromise. There could only be a bed for Mr. Romansky as a surgical admission.

The nightmare of Sanford's City Hospital experience had an odd effect on him. Before then, he had either been absolutely intractable or totally "out of it". Now he suddenly turned docile, cooperative, almost jovial. But that mood didn't last very long. His tempers again got the better of him. He became a disturbance to the patients around him and so utterly unmanageable for the staff that—for his own sake and for that of the institution—he would have to leave. The leg was doing fairly well and, in clear conscience, I felt that over a prolonged period with a modicum of care and a little luck, it might heal and permit him to get about.

And so Sanford was discharged. I arranged for one of our staff podiatrists to see him periodically and supervise his home care. When reports came back to me of slow but definite progess, I filled out his insurance papers, filed his chart, and Sanford lost his priority spot on my worry list.

A few weeks later Sanford's daughter came to my office with a recurrent bladder infection. "Everything all right with Dad?" I asked.

"Dad . . ." she hesitated, "Dad's at City Hospital . . . he's doing fine . . . getting over the operation." She saw the look on my face. The tears trickled down hers. Neither of us could speak. Finally the words came—"He just couldn't stand it at home. Don't you see . . . it's like I told you . . . ?"

Yes, I could see. Sanford Romansky had traded his gift from God—his swift and beloved leg—for a chrome and leather prop—anything—so that he could run clear of the hell of his life. He had sold the prize of his body to free what was left of his soul.

10

A Guide To The Perplexed
How To Choose Your Doctor

And well you might be perplexed by the almost daily torrents of conflictual reporting from the various tabernacles of medical research. Good food and bad food, sodium and sugar, calcium and cholesterol, vitamins, hormones and alcohol are all surveyed, analyzed and then either promoted or interdicted.

To futher confuse the do's and don't's of self-preservation, you may look to the lifestyles of the Europeans. Isn't it strange that the French pooh–pooh cholesterol levels under 300 while they merrily drink their wines and relish their butter and cheese laden diet? And why don't the English fuss about blood pressures unless they're over 180-200, and still get by with comparatively very little cardiac surgery? The Germans? They minimize all of our media-magnified advice and admonitions in favor of hot baths and long rest cure for health and longevity. Yet—with all these variations in living themes—the life expectancy figures are practically identical in all of the comparable developed countries of the world.

How do you thread your way through the minefields of puzzling data? Your neighbor, your barber or your well-meaning friends—all of whom are always quick to advise—are no better qualified than you. Only a physician is tooled and trained to sort through the maze and separate the wheat of legitimate medical research from the chaff of commercial promotion and to identify what is relevant for you.

The horse and buggy doctor, who was familiar with the souls and psyches as well as the bodies of every patient on his route, is long gone. But his contemporary replacement—the internist or the family practice physician—is available and should be central in patient management. Despite all you've read and heard, you cannot know whether your sudden unexplained weight loss belongs in the domain of the endocrinologist, the oncologist or the gastroenterologist. And, if you're troubled with a swollen gland, do you see a hematologist, an infectious disease expert or a general surgeon?

There is no question but that the specialists and the subspecialists, with their concentration on one field of medicine, have enhanced diagnostic and therapeutic techniques to the patient's benefit. However, the very nature of their work precludes their having the time or inclination to familiarize themselves with the total person—his genetic history, his frailties, his extra-medical complications. And that's what often limits their ability to mesh their sophisticated in-depth contribution into the whole picture.

So it is the internist or family practice physician who must be your primary resource, the prime mover for all health transport, the initiater of all referrals, the man in charge.

Choose this professional with care. Try to check out his reputation and his consulting room manner. Will he listen to you, level with you, relate to your problems? Inquire about his hospital affiliations. Top-notch physicians are generally associated with top-notch facilities that have access to top-notch specialists, consultants and equipment, in addition to top-notch care.

Having selected your capable and compatible medical advisor, let him translate your history, your examination and laboratory results into a language you can understand, be it in words of reassurance, caution or admonition. Let him advise you as to which specialized avenues you had best pursue. Let him determine the need for more intense investigation or treatment. Let him dissolve your amorphous fears. Let him be the guide for all your perplexities.

Note For Female Physicians:
Wherever, please read "she" for "he" and "her" for "him".

11

Cholesteromania

It's another year and yet another scare in the health arena. Intermittently, we've been belabored by the sugar scare, the red meat scare, the calcium scare—and now the cholesterol panic has taken over as the current national obsession. It's the new idiom of our speech, the buzz phrase at the cocktail party and the corner beer parlor, the country club and the assembly line. You are out of it if you don't have your "count" in your memory bank—along with your social security and your credit card numbers.

Documented studies by many well-recognized scientific groups underscore the advantages of a low blood cholesterol over a high one in terms of longevity, claiming that at present, 25 to 40 percent of our adult population is in jeopardy of devastating illness and premature death. Therefore they urge the lows to stay low and exhort the highs to reduce their levels via diet, exercise, and, if necessary, via drugs. I cannot argue these life-saving intentions nor the figures, but I must take exception to the way they've been promulgated for public consumption. This kind of foreboding message is fodder for the media who proceed to embellish it, dramatize it, and then preach it like gospel to an ever susceptible and fear-prone public. The prospect of an elevated cholesterol promising a bonafide invitation to calamity is nightmarish—even to the unapprehensive—and the resultant anxiety and

Published: *Cleveland Plain Dealer* May 3, 1988

fear may become more incapacitating than the questionable high cholesterol itself.

It was only a year or so ago that you were safe if your blood cholesterol level was under 280 milligrams percent, but now the cards have been reshuffled by the mega dealers in demographic research, and—with any number over 200—the deck is stacked against you. "Danger Ahead" is the signal; danger of atherosclerosis (hardening of the arteries) which, in turn, may ante the odds of a heart attack, a stroke, kidney failure and a hornet's nest of equally crippling or life threatening illnesses.

In my own practice of internal medicine we have always done blood studies, including cholesterol, as a part of our routine physical examinations. But, until they were converted into this new religion, patients never asked about their cholesterol count. Sugar? Frequently. Potassium? On occasion. Cholesterol? Never. The physician understands the vagaries and minor variations in the numbers expressed by a laboratory. The patient, however, ill-equipped to interpret them with any professional perspective, has the bejabbers scared out of him by what he reads and what he hears.

In this focus—I remember my parents' way of life and their eating modus. Bread was always slabbered with rich golden tub butter and coffee was always laced with heavy fresh cream. My mother loved to cook for her large family, and to her, no cake was worth baking unless it was made with a dozen eggs, and no beef was worth eating unless it was well-marbled. Neither of them was even conversant with aerobics or jogging, tennis or golf, or margarine. Yet they both died in their upper eighties, he of cancer of the prostate and she of late onset cerebrovascular disease. They were fortunate, I suppose, that they joyously lived out their lives never having to agonize over what they should and shouldn't eat. How blissful was their ignorance!

I do not say that an abnormally high blood cholesterol is an asset. I am decrying the arbitrary figures that seem to change with the seasons and tabulators. Obviously, isolated instances do not vitiate masses of statistics, but even solid data can be so mainipulated that it fails to consider the loopholes that many human numbers deserve. For example, it is positively proposed that "every 1% reduction in serum cholesterol level yields approximately a 2% reduction in coronary heart disease rate". Am I really to believe that lowering my own level down from 231 to 226 will reduce my risk of coronary artery disease by 10%? Really!

Despite the accented positivity of some of the "factual" reports, it must be noted that there is no unanimity amongst the authors and medical authorities on the significance of cholesterol in controlling one's health and influencing one's longevity. Currently, half of them disagree totally with theorizing about cholesterol and some even call it a form of "hysteria". Strangely, the dissertations of these dissenters never seem to be acknowledged or even mentioned in the lay literature. For example, the rather solid studies showing that moderate elevations of cholesterol has no effect on the longevity of people over fifty never gets coverage. It appears that only the dramatically bad stuff gets through to the public eye and ear.

And, isn't it strange that –in the tempest of cholesterol propaganda—the genetic factor in the development of atherosclerosis seldom surfaces. We know that there are some people who inherit the tendency to form early and severe hardening of the arteries and are therefore prone to strokes and heart attacks regardless of what they eat, what they do, or what level of blood cholesterol they carry. Yes, taking dietary steps and staying thin and active may help, but—by and large—the risk factor in this group exceeds even that of the carefree bon vivant. Unfortunately, we have no options in the choice of our parents, and, in our present state of knowledge, the physician can only recognize the problem with limited tools, then cope with it as he must with other inherited diseases.

In the ivory towers of institutional research, many new frontiers have been opened and much has been discovered for the benefit of mankind over the years. Neither the motivations of investigational science nor it's accomplishments should be demeaned or minimized. It is a fact, however, that in recent years, much of this work has been and is still subsidized by grants, many of which are funded by pharmaceutical companies. These companies have a proprietary interest in developing, manufacturing, and selling cholesterol lowering drugs. The market analysts have projected a 5 to 10 billion dollar return per year for the sale of cholesterol related drugs, making it big, big business. The thrust of their promotion is fanning the flames of fear in anyone or everyone with a number over the magic "200", and then offering them their name brand of "quick fix"—for a price. And, mixed in with this army of mercenaries are the Washington lobbyists, who, under the "Hurray for Good Health and Long Life" banner, are fighting the age old battle of what comes first, the chicken (low cholesterol) or the egg (high cholesterol).

So—how do I handle my long time patient, a little octogenarian lady who recently booked an appointment just to have her cholesterol checked? Yes, she sheepishly admitted, she was feeling as fine as always and frankly, didn't have the vaguest notion of what cholesterol was, but the "medical experts" in her Tuesday bridge game insisted she find out the number, because—should it be over 200—they assured her she'd be in for big trouble.

And how about another of my regulars—a delightful old gentleman who apologized for calling, but explained that his daughter, Gertrude, had insisted. She had just read an article about cholesterol and remembered my telling her father at his last examination that his count was 242. *Now* she was convinced that was dangerous so, "Quick call the doctor and find out how many eggs you can eat". "Papa" is 92 years old, still plays golf, and never counted eggs before. Do the Gertrudes of this world want immortality for their loved ones? Do they really devour all the baloney that's put out for public consumption?

As physicians, we have an obligation to encourage and foster good health measures and educate the general public on how best to live in our environment. We must try to allay confusion and fear in our patients by clarifying variant and unproven data for them. So often, this year's "fact" becomes next year's "theory", and the year after, it can fade into a fallen "concept". That perspective must be shared with those who depend on us.

And, as physicians, we must conscientiously try to defuse the media's bold and uncontested bombardment of health information. If we do not protest this unprofessional glut, we are renegade to our calling. If we just stand by and let it happen, we are accomplices in the crime of perpetrating anxiety in a generation that is already stress-ridden and pock-marked with neuroses.

12
The Practice of Medicine— A Half Century

Having lived within the self-imposed, but rather constrictive confines of a medical career for half a century, I feel the need, like the prisoner of old, to carve into the walls of my cell a few observations and words of guidance for the poor unfortunates who are to follow me. Unlike Winston Churchill, who said his life had been an exciting voyage, but one he would not care to repeat, I would love to relive mine, because for me the practice of medicine has always been an exhilirating, challenging and satisfying pursuit. My generation had the extreme good fortune of living through the truly halcyon days of medicine. In our fifty years, we were both audience and players in the greatest and most exciting drama in the entire history of our calling—the explosive development of a solid science out of a tattered group of hand-me-down facts and fancies.

When we started in medical school, we were subjected to a brutal memory process of diagnosis, disease and drugs, and withal, became versed in the jargon of the profession. By the end of four years, we had acquired a rather crude overview of the differences between sick and well, but the treatments we were offered were woefully lacking. We had learned the names and dosages of a great number of palliative drugs, but in essence, there were only a few worthy staples on the shelf: digitalis, morphine, quinine, belladonna

Address; 50th Reunion—Georgetown Medical School—June–1990
Published: *Cleveland Plain Dealer*—June 29, 1990.

and aspirin. Surgery was potentially curative, but we medical people were so limited that even a serious infection like pneumonia was treated by swabbing down the fever and providing lots of fresh air. Oh yes, we were taught about the noble heritage of the healing arts, the dignity of the body and the sanctity of the human mind and spirit. We were instructed in ethics and pride and morality. We were taught to be kind and caring and, above all, to do no harm. Yes, there was honor and striving in our group, but what we really started with when we left these hallowed halls, were some vague projections; the laying on of hands, a willing ear, some kind reassuring words and a dignified professional air.

Shortly after our graduation, our world began to change. Antibiotics and antisera were discovered and started to proliferate in dizzying procession; saddling and taming the ravaging infectious diseases so that an illness-free millenium seemed to be just around the corner. Nature, however, can be a tricky adversary. Germs soon developed resistance and new forms appeared. Even now, although the new and mysterious miasma that is AIDS has come over the horizon and threatens to envelop us in its deadly embrace, and a new and potent global flu could suddenly explode to scourge and plague us, we *have* made dramatic progress in the treatment of the infectious diseases.

You and I really have lived through many wondrous changes in medicine. We have seen Kolff's dialysis machines made small enough and practical enough to be used universally to rescue end-stage renal disease patients from what formerly had been a death sentence.

We have marvelled as the heart became an open book—on the angiography table and in the operating room. New vessels and new valves can now turn back the human odometers on many a dead-end road.

The development of fiber optics has taken the word "rigid" out of endoscopy, and made it possible for us to navigate the curls and convolutions of the lung and the G.I. tract—plucking their polyps on the way.

The nitrogen mustards, conceived as satanic dealers of death during war time, have been tempered, harnessed and converted into angels of mercy for the treatment of lymphomas, leukemia, and cancer.

We have learned how to replace steamy worn-out lenses almost as easily as changing batteries in a toy, and, we can toy with the batteries of our cardiac pacemakers.

With the growth and development of computers and scanners, we are now able to find the proverbial needle in the diagnostic haystack, and with guided needle biopsy, the guesswork has been taken out of many previously puzzling disorders, making pinpoint therapy a possiblility.

The crutches and braces that used to hang in rows in the storerooms of the orthopedic departments, now have been replaced by a wide assortment of gleaming new hips, new knees, new elbows, and new shoulders.

We are living in a new and wonderful world of medicine—replete with magical machines and miraculous therapeutic tools and techniques to relieve pain and prolong life. However, there is a catch. All of the paraphenalia in this exotic arsenal are just as costly to space and to operate, as they are to buy. Only highly trained technicians can run them and only very specialized physicians can interpret them. In addition, these megabuck machines become obsolete within months and need to be replaced with improved versions for more millions. The 2 and 3 dollar medical visits of the 1940s have skyed to hundreds of dollars, and hospital costs have soared to multiple thousands. The practice of medicine has become big business and in many of our specialties, disproportionately lucrative. The pot of medical honey has gotten so full and so sweet that it has enticed all the big time predators; business advisors, soothsayers, machinery makers, drug peddlers, and the media who have jumped in to keep the pot boiling. By a kind of natural accretion, we have acquired a vast overlay of nonmedical people who are blanketing the entire kaleidoscope of the life and function of medical practice. In addition, with the tremendous input of third party payment, there is a countless cast of nonpracticing physicians, nurses, attorneys, insurance brokers and executives, business consultants and many others—reviewing, censoring, controlling—all feeding at the trough of the medical dollar. This ancillary intrusion on the physician adds immeasurably to the overall "cost of medical care", but in no way contributes to the actual care of a single patient. And so it is the patient who is penalized by the escalating costs, costs that never enhance the quality of his care. There must be a way to scrape these barnacles off our hull before their very weight will cause us to capsize and sink.

Just as all of America has changed in the last fifty years, the kindly old painstaking physician has had to become more worldly and business-wise to survive. The family "Doc" has been replaced by the medical corporation, busily harvesting and investing in accordance with the best corporate diligence and business know-how. Although the majority of our fellows still hew to the drawn ethical lines of the profession, there are too many who have detoured from Hippocrates to hype, from caring to coining—which, unfortunately, besmirches the whole fraternity in the eyes of the public. We cannot go back to the horse and buggy nor even to the Fords of the 40s, but we must try to rededicate oursleves to the concept that the patient and his needs belong higher up on the totem pole of our social structure than they are at present. We must not allow the proliferating entrepreneurial trappings in medicine today to compromise the noble heritage of the profession to which we dedicated ourselves 50 years ago.